MW00334503

THE MERGER MYSTERY

The Merger Mystery

Why Spend Ever More on Mergers When So Many Fail?

Geoff Meeks and J. Gay Meeks

https://www.openbookpublishers.com

© 2022 Geoff Meeks and J. Gay Meeks

This work is licensed under a Creative Commons Attribution-NonCommercial-NoDerivatives 4.0 International license (CC BY-NC-ND 4.0). This license allows you to share, copy, distribute and transmit the work for non-commercial purposes, providing attribution is made to the author (but not in any way that suggests that he endorses you or your use of the work). Attribution should include the following information:

Geoff Meeks and J. Gay Meeks, *The Merger Mystery: Why Spend Ever More on Mergers When So Many Fail?* Cambridge, UK: Open Book Publishers, 2022, https://doi.org/10.11647/OBP.0309

Copyright and permissions for the reuse of many of the images included in this publication differ from the above. This information is provided in the captions and in the list of illustrations.

In order to access detailed and updated information on the license, please visit https://doi.org/10.11647/OBP.0309#copyright. Further details about CC BY-NC-ND licenses are available at http://creativecommons.org/licenses/by-nc-nd/4.0/

All external links were active at the time of publication unless otherwise stated and have been archived via the Internet Archive Wayback Machine at https://archive.org/web

Digital material and resources associated with this volume are available at https://doi.org/10.11647/OBP.0309#resources

Every effort has been made to identify and contact copyright holders and any omission or error will be corrected if notification is made to the publisher.

ISBN Paperback: 9781800647794
ISBN Hardback: 9781800647800
ISBN Digital (PDF): 9781800647817
ISBN Digital ebook (EPUB): 9781800647824
ISBN Digital ebook (AZW3): 9781800647831
ISBN XML: 9781800647848
ISBN HTML: 9781800647855
DOI: 10.11647/OBP.0309

Cover image: *Chitten* by Arne Olav Gurvin Fredriksen, https://www.gyyporama.com/
Cover design by Katy Saunders and J. Gay Meeks.

Contents

Author Biographies   ix

Preface   xi

Acknowledgements   xv

List of Abbreviations   xvii

PART ONE: INTRODUCING THE MYSTERY   **1**

1. The Challenge   3

    Mergers that Succeed   3

    First-hand Experience   7

    Post-merger Performance: Further Statistical Analysis   9

    The Mystery Emerges   10

    One Apparent Solution   11

    What Counts as Success or Failure in Merger?   13

    Plan of the Book   17

PART TWO: DETECTION: FOLLOWING THE CLUES   **19**

Section A: Misaligned Incentives for Executives,
Advisers and Others   **21**

2. Incentives for Executives   23

    Pay   23

    Perks: Benefits in Kind   27

    Power and Protection   28

    Prestige   30

3. Incentives for Advisers 33

The Scale of Advisers' Fees in M&A Transactions 33

The Dilemma for the Adviser 35

A Surprising Insight into How Much Work Expert Advisers
Sometimes Do on a Deal 36

The Revised Sequence 39

Special Purpose Acquisition Companies (SPACs) 40

Other Perks for the Advice Industry 41

4. Incentives for Other Participants 45

Non-executive Directors 45

Fund Managers 46

Academic Experts 48

*Section B: Distorted Financial Engineering: Moral Hazard,
Tax Privileges and Private Equity* **49**

5. Moral Hazard 51

Magnifying Earnings with Debt Finance 51

Limited Liability and Moral Hazard 52

Free Loans from Suppliers 54

Free Loans from Pensioners 54

6. Subsidies for Merging Firms 57

Subsidising Corporate Debt Used to Fund Merger: Tax-deductible
Interest 57

Using Merger to Convert Income into More Lightly Taxed Capital
Gains 58

International Tax Arbitrage via M&A 59

Annexe to Chapter 6 61

7. Private Equity (PE) 63

Managing Acquired Businesses 64

Financial Engineering 64

Incentives for Top PE Executives 66

Section C: Information Asymmetry **69**

8. Inefficient Mergers in an 'Efficient' Market   71
    Theory   71
    Evidence   73

9. The Accountant's M&A Cookbook   77
    Creative Accounting ahead of the Offer   79
    Great Expectations: Forecasts of Post-merger Earnings   83
    Accounting for the Deal: Creating Spurious Post-merger
    Earnings   84
    Creative Accounting Post-merger   85
    The Intangibles Anomaly   87

10. Feedback Loops   89

PART THREE: RESOLUTION: REVIEW AND REFORM   **93**

11. Exemplars of Failure   95
    Carillion   95
    GE   100

12. Remedies?   103
    Curbing Rent Extraction Arising from Distorted Financial
    Engineering   105
    Reducing Information Asymmetry   109
    Better Aligning Incentives   111

Appendix 1: Measuring Success or Failure   115
    Time Frames   116
    Acquirer and Target   118
    Other Things Equal   118
    Examples   118

Appendix II: Managing Earnings around M&A   123
    Ahead of an Offer   123
    Accounting for the Deal   127

Accounting Post-merger   130

A Step Too Far: Accounting for Merger to Conceal
a Management Failure   132

References   135

Index   155

   Index of Businesses   155

   Subject Index   156

Author Biographies

Geoff Meeks is Emeritus Professor and Senior Research Associate at the Judge Business School, University of Cambridge, where he has served as Professor of Financial Accounting, Head of the Finance and Accounting Group, Director of Teaching, Director of Research, and Acting Dean. His previous positions were at Price Waterhouse, Edinburgh University, and the Cambridge Economics Faculty, where he was Director of Graduate Studies. He has been Visiting Scholar at Harvard Business School, INSEAD, and London School of Economics, and has held a Fellowship at Darwin College, Cambridge and an Academic Fellowship at the Institute of Chartered Accountants in England and Wales.

J. Gay Meeks is Senior Research Associate in the Centre of Development Studies, University of Cambridge. Her previous positions were at St. Anne's College, Oxford and in the Cambridge Economics Faculty. She has taught Moral Philosophy at the University of Glasgow; served as Fellow and Director of Studies in Economics at Robinson College, Cambridge; and won Cambridge's Student-led Lecturer of the Year Award for 2016–2017 for her M Phil course.

Preface

Across the world, several trillion dollars—equivalent to the national income of the whole German economy—are now spent on mergers and acquisitions (M&A) each year. 2021 broke all records, with well over $5trillion of investors' money devoted to M&A. Yet, surprisingly, statistical studies over the last four decades suggest that, although some mergers are positive-sum, very many do not lead to increased operating profits.

Of course, it is to be expected that—as with any investment decision—managers' weaknesses and mistakes (as well as bad luck) would lead to some failures. But over time you would expect managers and their advisers to learn from their mistakes, filter out unpromising mergers, and ensure that a large majority of deals result in operating gains. However, this has not happened. M&A activity has continued to grow: globally there are some forty times more deals each year now than there were forty years ago. And the gains in operating profit are as elusive as ever. 'Anyone who has researched merger success rates knows that roughly 70% fail,' argued leading consultancy, McKinsey.

It is not that the M&A industry is short of talent. On the contrary, some of the brightest and most profit-motivated graduates of leading universities and business schools beat a path to the M&A departments of investment banks, consultancies, and law firms, or to businesses whose strategy is built on M&A.

So the 'merger mystery' is that, under present arrangements it is to be expected that talented, energetic, highly skilled, law-abiding, income-maximising participants in the M&A market will continue to promote mergers which often lead to no operating gains—seemingly strange behaviour that is liable to have adverse effects on the wider economy.

Answers to the mystery, we contend, can be detected in misaligned incentives, distorted financial engineering, and information asymmetry.

In support of this argument we present a synthesis of the ideas of economists from Adam Smith to modern Nobel Laureates, findings from over a hundred peer-reviewed statistical studies, and case evidence from many businesses—again over a hundred—involved in merger.

This evidence is chiefly for the UK and US, whose M&A markets have historically been the most active. But we include material from other regions, where M&A activity is 'catching up'.

Although the book's argument is based on technical material from economics, finance and accounting, we have aimed to make it accessible to anyone—practitioner, investor, student, journalist, politician, academic—who feels comfortable reading the business sections of the serious press, and is interested in the M&A stories which feature so prominently in those sections. We leave a trail to original sources for those who want to delve further.

Critics of this book—especially those who make a living from M&A—will no doubt complain that it is selective and one-sided. They might say it gives insufficient weight to those mergers that succeed. But our focus is deliberate. The bookstores, company documents and media hagiographies are awash with material on the upside of M&A—the success stories. And some of this material is very good. But analysis of M&A <u>failure</u> is under-represented—not commensurate with its extent and its economic and social damage.

The very first section of the book highlights potential sources of private and social benefit from merger and gives success stories. But thereafter it turns to situations which fail to deliver operating gains. So the book counteracts the overwhelmingly positive tone of most of the commentary on M&A. And it concentrates on areas where there is hope of improvement—where a set of reforms in taxation, regulation and participants' contracts are suggested which we believe could reduce significantly the number of mergers that fail.

We expect a further set of rebukes from experts in the several professions and academic disciplines we bring together, including accounting, central banking, corporate law, finance, governance, industrial economics, and investment banking. They will be offended that we have strayed into their territory, and object that we have neglected important detail. Our defence is that our broad overview helps to reveal how weaknesses at multiple points interact and cumulate to produce inefficient outcomes.

This book focuses on the economic efficiency of M&A. The distributional aspects of merger activity which are also evident here will be explored further in a sister study, 'Rising Inequality: The Contribution of Corporate Merger'.

Acknowledgements

We are very grateful to the following experts who have read part or all of a draft of the book and given us valuable corrections and suggestions: Amir Amel-Zadeh, Tim Bellis, Allan Cook, Gishan Dissanaike, Jonathan Faasse, Polly Meeks, Simon Taylor, and anonymous publisher's reviewers. Of course, they bear no responsibility for the outcome.

Ha-Joon Chang, Bart Lambrecht, and Christoph Loch provided a very supportive research environment as Directors of Cambridge's Centre for Development Studies, Centre for Finance, and Judge Business School respectively.

We have benefitted greatly from the contributions of the OBP team— editors Alessandra Tosi and Melissa Purkiss, as well as Luca Baffa, Laura Rodriguez Pupo and Katy Saunders.

Our thanks also go to Arne Fredriksen for kind permission to use his hybrid animal collage 'Chitten' on the cover.

List of Abbreviations

AAA	American Accounting Association
ASB	Accounting Standards Board (UK)
ASBJ	Accounting Standards Board of Japan
BIG4	Major accounting/audit firms: Deloitte, EY, KPMG, PwC
bn	billion
CAPEX	Spending on buying, maintaining, or improving fixed assets such as land, buildings and equipment
'Carry'	Carried interest (private equity)
CEO	Chief executive officer
CFO	Chief financial officer
EC	European Commission
EMH	Efficient markets hypothesis
EPS	Earnings per share
FASB	Financial Accounting Standards Board (US)
FCA	Financial Conduct Authority (UK)
FRS	Financial Reporting Standard (UK)
FT	*Financial Times*
FTSE	Financial Times Stock Exchange (100 Index) (UK)
GDP	Gross domestic product
GNH	Gross national happiness
HDI	Human development index
HoC	House of Commons (UK Parliament)
HQ	Headquarters
IASB	International Accounting Standards Board
IP	Intellectual property
IPO	Initial public offering (of shares)
LSE	London Stock Exchange
M&A	Mergers and acquisitions
mn	million
NED	Non-executive director
NRV	Net realizable value
OECD	Organisation for Economic Cooperation and Development

P&L	Profit and loss account
PE	Price-to-earnings ratio
PE	Private Equity
PR	Public relations
PRP	Performance-related pay
R&D	Research and development
SEC	Securities and Exchange Commission (US)
SPAC	Special purpose acquisition company
tn	trillion
TSR	Total shareholder return
WSJ	*Wall Street Journal*

PART ONE

INTRODUCING THE MYSTERY

1. The Challenge

Anyone who has researched merger success rates knows that roughly 70% fail. (McKinsey 2010)

Globally there have been some 40,000 mergers a year recently compared with about a thousand 40 years ago. (Amel-Zadeh and Meeks 2020a)

Mergers[1] that Succeed

In our college days, the economics tradition was pretty confident about the outcome to be expected from merger and acquisition. Adam Smith, the revered grandfather of modern economics,[2] while not addressing M&A directly (there was scarcely any at the time), had in 1776 identified potential sources of gain which are standard elements of merger proposals today: securing scale economies, replacing weak management, and enhancing market power.

He drew attention to the scale economies which could be achieved through the division of labour when small-scale production was replaced by larger factory organisations. In his famous example of the pin factory, output per man per day for the individual pin-maker working at home was 24 pins (Pratten 1980), whereas his counterpart in a 1776 factory with specialised functions produced 4,800 pins.[3] Greater scale through consolidation brought lower unit cost.[4]

---

1   We follow common practice in using the terms merger, acquisition, takeover, M&A, and combination interchangeably. In some specialist contexts—such as accounting—they are differentiated.
2   Revered by economists from both orthodox and heterodox persuasions, albeit with contrasting interpretations of some aspects of his approach.
3   By 1980 increasing scale was associated with a rise to 800,000 pins per person per day.
4   But probably not without some painful processes of adjustment.

© 2022 Geoff Meeks and J. Gay Meeks, CC BY-NC-ND 4.0   https://doi.org/10.11647/OBP.0309.01

A twenty-first century example is offered by the vehicle manufacturer Volkswagen. After a string of acquisitions, including Audi, Porsche, Scania, Seat and Skoda, it was the world's biggest producer of vehicles—some 10 million a year. Shared components for the different subsidiaries could be produced in specialised units at unprecedented scale and reduced cost. Likewise, the fruits of R&D could be shared across the combine.

The second feature Smith (1776/1937) drew attention to was a characteristic of the emerging modern economy of joint stock companies where management was separated from ownership:

> The directors of such [joint-stock] companies, however, being the managers rather of other people's money than of their own, it cannot well be expected that they should watch over it with the same anxious vigilance with which the partners in a private co-partnery frequently watch over their own... Negligence and profusion, therefore, must always prevail, more or less, in the management of the affairs of such a company. (p. 700).

This problem—which nowadays goes under the heading of the 'principal-agent', or 'corporate governance', or 'stewardship' problem that arises when management is divorced from ownership—also suggested an opportunity. A potential source of profit from M&A, and gain in economic efficiency, would result from a 'turnaround' merger, where stronger management gained control of an underperforming firm, boosting its profit and increasing its valuation. 'The potential return from the successful takeover and revitalization of a poorly run company can be enormous', wrote Manne (1965, p. 113).

A few miles from Adam Smith's birthplace near Edinburgh, another Scotsman, Fred Goodwin, proved himself expert in this mode of M&A two centuries later. As head of Royal Bank of Scotland, he secured massive gains for the shareholders by firing 18,000 employees after he acquired NatWest Bank, earning the nickname 'Fred the Shred'. The acquisition was meticulously planned and ruthlessly delivered. Staff held to be under-performing were removed and backroom functions combined, yielding within two years an increase of over 70% in earnings per share and over 100% in the RBS share price.[5] His

---

5   Reference for Business (2022).

continued acquisition activities built the largest bank in the world.[6] And M&A earned him more than money—the much-coveted British honour bestowed by the Queen: a knighthood.[7]

In the United States—which lost its monarch in 1776, the very year of Adam Smith's great work—it might be held that *Fortune* magazine awards the honours instead. And the greatest accolade in its gift was reserved for Jack Welch, who, by the end of last century, built GE into the world's biggest corporation.[8] *Fortune* named him 'manager of the century' in 1999. Through a series of almost one thousand acquisitions over two decades he transformed an engineering business into a conglomerate whose activities ranged from broadcasting to finance. His nickname was 'Neutron Jack'—like the neutron bomb, he got rid of people while leaving the surroundings intact. In shedding labour he adopted the formula employed for the armies of classical Rome, routinely 'decimating' 10% in the event of failure. Managers of new acquisitions had to rank the performance of their underlings, and the bottom 10% were fired if they did not improve.[9] In the two decades from 1980 GE's earnings rose from $1.5 billion to almost $13 billion, and the stock price rose even faster.

The acquisitions by Volkswagen, RBS and GE were unequivocally successful at the time for the owners of the businesses. However, establishing whether an acquisition was successful from the perspective of the whole economy requires a more complicated calculation, discussed later in this chapter and in Appendix 1. The gist is that conventional measures of returns to shareholders typically overstate the gains (understate the losses) in operating efficiency. And further, standard measures of operating efficiency typically overstate the gains (understate the losses) to the economy at large. In the larger context, success depends on whether any gains to the owners have just come at the expense of other interest groups. Merger outcome in general may be positive-, zero- or negative-sum, and the discussion later in this

---

6 By assets in 2008.
7 The reputations of Fred the Shred and Neutron Jack subsequently declined. See Chapter 3 on the former, Gryta and Mann (2020) on the latter.
8 Measured by stock market capitalisation.
9 Gryta and Mann (2020). This applied to existing activities too, and more than 100,000 jobs were cut in the 1980s alone (p. 18).

book concerns the pattern of gains and losses from merger for different interest groups.

Scale economies and more efficient utilisation of labour potentially offer positive-sum outcomes for the economy as a whole[10]—fewer inputs are required to create the same outputs, or better outputs for the same inputs. But the third source of gain from merger foreshadowed by Adam Smith (1776/1937) is often deemed negative-sum. He noted that:

> People of the same trade seldom meet together, even for merriment and diversion, but the conversation ends in a conspiracy against the public, or in some contrivance to raise prices (p. 128)

The smaller the number of people in 'the same trade', the easier it is to raise prices. One way of looking at this is through a game theory lens (see, for instance Hannah and Kay 1977). A pure monopolist should be able to extract the maximum possible profits from a market. Oligopolists who share a market might collectively enjoy those maximum profits if they cooperate—in a formal or tacit cartel—to mimic the price and output solution for the monopoly. But individual members of the cartel could gain by cheating, against the group's interests, for example by offering under-the-counter discounts—provided that they could avoid detection and retaliation. The probability of detection and the impact of retaliation are likely to be higher the fewer firms supply the market: eliminating rivals via M&A offers an oligopolist the prospect of greater collusion and of securing higher prices and profits.

The US airline industry offers a striking modern example of M&A being used as 'a contrivance to raise prices'—enhancing market power and transforming profits. For most of the hundred years since the original flight at Kitty Hawk, the industry had a dismal history of financial performance. Legendary investor Warren Buffett of Berkshire Hathaway, the 'Sage of Omaha', explained the background in characteristically colourful terms:

> The worst sort of business is one that grows rapidly, requires significant capital to engender the growth, and then earns little or no money. Think airlines. Here a durable competitive advantage has proven elusive ever since the days of the Wright Brothers. Indeed, if a farsighted capitalist

---

10   This assumes a buoyant economy in which employees can readily find new jobs.

had been present at Kitty Hawk, he would have done his successors a huge favor by shooting Orville down. (Buffett 1982)

In an interview in 1999, Buffett said: 'As of 1992 [...] the money that had been made since the dawn of aviation by all of this country's airline companies was zero. Absolutely zero' (Buffett 1999).

Things went from bad to worse after the millennium: the years between 2000 and the financial crash of 2008 saw the US airline industry make further cumulative losses of some $60 billion (Dissanaike, Jayasekera and Meeks 2022).

But then the 'people of the same trade' (airlines) did 'meet together' in a series of mergers: Delta and Northwest in 2008; United and Continental in 2010; Southwest and AirTran in 2010; and American Airlines and US Airways in 2013. The four mergers together resulted in a 4-firm oligopoly within the domestic US industry controlling more than 80% of domestic capacity. Even this measure understates their market power—individual members of the oligopoly tended to dominate local hubs: at 40 of the biggest 100 US airports a single airline accounted for the majority of business (Tepper and Hearn 2019, p. xiv). As textbook theory of monopoly predicts, output was cut back and prices increased (a negative effect on general economic efficiency). But the firms themselves gained: the number of flights was cut even as passenger numbers increased—leaving fewer empty seats. Margins widened, and the airline industry's fortunes were turned round: profits for 2009–2017 summed to $75 billion. Even Warren Buffett invested $10 billion in the airlines (Dissanaike et al. 2022).

First-hand Experience

So when one of us joined an audit firm whose clients were especially active in M&A, we knew what to expect. We would witness the stimulus to profit from M&A which featured in our college economic theory and in the media tales of conquests by heroic managers.

Working as an auditor may well be the closest you can get to being the proverbial fly on the wall. You sit in the client's office for weeks on end, with access to the books, watching their employees at work, and—better than the fly on the wall—you are able to ask questions. However, auditing is famous for its deleterious effect on mental health. Mostly the damage comes from acute boredom as you review endless tables of numbers—combined with the antipathy of the client's staff whose work you are scrutinising. But in this case, acting as auditor to businesses which had recently been taken over produced acute cognitive dissonance. There was a clash between economic theory and media hagiographies on the one side, and mundane experience in the field on the other. The abiding memory is of cuts in the budgets for staff, investment, maintenance and marketing; of fearful, demoralised employees; of shrinking sales; and of profits flat or in decline.

Given this cognitive dissonance in auditing, the choice of question for one of our PhDs, which followed life as an auditor, was obvious. If the financial performance of a population of acquiring firms was traced, would it conform to the great expectations engendered by a training in economics and the media tales of heroic leaders, or would it reflect the post-marital problems of the merging firms just observed on the front line?

With IT still at a primitive stage, assembling and standardising the accounts for a population of hundreds of acquirers and their targets, adjusting for accounting biases and controlling for other influences on profits was a laborious job. The resulting book, whose conclusion was presented in the title—*Disappointing Marriage: A Study of the Gains from Merger* (Meeks 1977)—and was further developed in journal papers,[11] elicited a range of responses. Economist colleagues were dismissive of the finding that, *on average*, M&A had not enhanced profits ('quite implausible—inconsistent with basic economics: haven't you read Adam Smith and the literatures on scale economies, market power and turnaround takeover?'). Those who made a living from M&A rejected the results angrily: the review by one professional M&A adviser memorably described the book as 'a farrago of nonsense'.

In the light of these responses from the experts we might have retired ignominiously from this field. But unsolicited reassurance that we may not just have made silly measurement errors came from the Editor of the *Financial Times*, who said it chimed with his experience. He was head of one of the most formidable intelligence-gathering operations in world business, one we draw on extensively in the following chapters. And

---

11   Meeks and Meeks, 1981a, 1981b.

the UK government were also more open-minded in their response: in a Green Paper (HMSO 1978), they summarised this book and other evidence, concluding that it constituted 'a strong challenge to the previous presumption that the great majority of mergers confer economic benefits' (p. 105).

Post-merger Performance: Further Statistical Analysis

The subsequent four decades have seen many studies which could have given the lie to our early attempts at measuring the impact of M&A on financial performance. Appendix 1 summarises briefly several dozen peer-reviewed articles and books on this aspect of the subject. Unsurprisingly, there is considerable variety of coverage and approach among them. They adopt different methodologies and rely on different data—some on accounting profits, others on share prices. They try different ways of controlling for other influences on performance. They relate to 10 different countries (though the US dominates, with the UK a strong runner-up). And they cover many different time periods over the last half-century.

No more than our original studies do they show that all M&A has produced the disappointing outcomes one of us observed at some of our audit clients: there are many deals that—along with those by Volkswagen, RBS, GE, and US airlines—have produced significant gains to shareholders. But taken together they do suggest that the central tendency is disappointing. Only a fifth of the studies report that in the mergers they investigated, the average deal, or a majority of deals, produced higher profits for the combined firms, or increased the wealth of the acquirers' shareholders. The one reliably bright spot is that, in general, target shareholders gain from a premium price paid by the acquirer, but often this is outweighed by the losses to the acquirers' shareholders: it is a 'negative-sum' outcome even if we don't count the effect on interest groups other than shareholders—the frequent losses to customers, suppliers, employees, lenders, pensioners and taxpayers that we document in later chapters.

One of the most ambitious studies of financial accounts relating to M&A in the US (Ravenscraft and Scherer 1987) had special access to data, allowing the authors to follow the accounts of targets within the new combinations. They concluded (p. 193ff.) that 'one third of all acquisitions were subsequently sold off [...] On average merged lines later sold off had a negative operating income during the last year before they were resold. Among the survivors, profitability also tended to decline...'; and, surprisingly, their results were often corroborated by the executives who had initiated the deals when they were interviewed by the economists. A subsequent major US study of the effect of acquisition announcements on the share prices of US acquirers in the course of a four-year merger wave (Moeller et al. 2005). was entitled 'Wealth Destruction on a Massive Scale [...]'. It found a loss of 12 cents per dollar spent on M&A—a total loss of $240 bn. Target firm shareholders gained—the bidder usually has to offer a premium to gain control—but bidders' losses exceeded targets' gains by $134 bn. In a very recent study (Amel-Zadeh and Meeks 2020a) we charted the total shareholder return[12] of larger US acquirers in the two years following all 4,450 significant acquisitions with a deal value exceeding $100 million completed in the period 2002–2017. Relative to matched non-acquirers, they suffered a loss—of 5.3% on average over the period as a whole: in only three of the fifteen years was there an average gain.[13]

The Mystery Emerges

The mystery we are exploring in this book is that, as this evidence of disappointing results from M&A accumulated, more and more acquisition activity was initiated. Since the early disappointing results were published some four decades ago, the global total of M&A transactions each year has risen to more than 40,000 in every year from 2006 to 2018.[14] Spending on M&A reached $4 trillion in every year from 2014 to 2018, and 2021 broke all records.

When reading about financial markets, it is easy to become inured to numbers which end in a string of zeros. We need some standard of comparison. How significant are these numbers in relation to the

---

12   Dividends plus share price appreciation relative to equity.
13   This is despite the increased opportunities in recent years to gain from debt-financed acquisitions as a result of the monetary authorities manipulating the debt market and the tax authorities continuing to privilege debt finance (Chapters 5 and 6 below).
14   Amel-Zadeh and Meeks (2020a, p. 2) provide the main data in this paragraph.

resources available to potential acquirers? Seventy years ago, growth by M&A was a relatively insignificant aspect of strategy, and presumably consumed little of the time and energy of senior executives and their boards. In the US the 1900 peak in such activity was not reached again until the 1960s, antitrust legislation having been introduced in the meantime (Scherer and Ross 1990, p. 154). Spending by listed firms on M&A in 1950s UK was equal to only around 15% of spending on new fixed assets; but it grew rapidly in the sixties.[15] Two Credit Suisse studies (Mauboussin and Callahan 2014, 2015) compare aggregate M&A spending with CAPEX (capital expenditure devoted to buying, maintaining, or improving fixed assets such as land, buildings or machines) from 1980 to 2013 for the US, Europe and Asia Pacific. In the West, M&A caught up with CAPEX and then overtook it, reaching two or three times CAPEX in cyclical peaks.[16] In the East, apart from Japan, the trends were in the same direction but less pronounced.

So, as evidence of disappointing outcomes mounted, Western businesses were devoting to M&A a large and rapidly increasing share of their key strategic resources: investment funds and senior executives' time and energy.[17]

One Apparent Solution

At first sight, one important strand of writing seems to offer an explanation of the failure of so many mergers to reap the operating gains which scale economies, enhanced market power and turnaround mergers would

---

15 Meeks (1977). It briefly even overtook spending on new fixed assets in 1968, a spike year for promiscuous couplings of humans too in the 'Year of Turmoil and Change' (Archives.gov).

16 CAPEX has, of course, been growing relatively slowly in recent decades as new industries have invested more heavily in intangible assets (see Chapter 9 below).

17 Another feature which will be strategic in unraveling the puzzle is that executives have been focusing not just on the prospect of making acquisitions, but also on the possibility of themselves becoming takeover targets. M&A has become by far the most common cause of corporate 'death'. Of the population of larger companies listed on UK stock exchanges in 1948, 83% had been taken over by 2018 (Meeks and Whittington 2021). In the US, the number of businesses listed on the Stock Exchange has roughly halved since 1996 (Tepper and Hearn 2019), mostly as a result of merger. Sometimes businesses have merged or made acquisitions in order to 'stay alive' themselves—avoiding becoming a target. For example, Kynaston (2001, p. 387) describes the bosses of two major retail banks in the UK, National Provincial and Westminster, agreeing to merge to create 'a bank that would be too big to be taken over by anyone else'.

seem to offer. This explanation emphasises diseconomies of scale, and the difficulties executives face when expanding rapidly through merger.

There is a long-established literature on the diseconomies of scale in business. One strand focuses on the growing distance between the CEO and the 'front line' of production and marketing as businesses expand and reporting lines multiply (Robinson 1931). A related strand focuses on the difficulty of coordinating the different parts of a large organisation. Scherer and Ross (1990) write that 'Hordes of middle managers, coordinators, and expediters proliferate' (p. 104), helpfully adding an explanatory footnote: 'For readers untutored in the ways of bureaucracy, an expediter is a person whose desk is between the desks of two coordinators'.

Compelling accounts of the challenges executives might encounter in the acquisition process are provided in, for example, the early theoretical work of Penrose (1959) and Marris (1963), and the empirical studies of Ravenscraft and Scherer (1987) and Fernandes (2019). Penrose emphasised the difficulties of assimilating large additions to the management team. Other challenges include evaluating the gains to be secured from an acquisition, identifying obstacles to achieving those gains, and devising plans to overcome those obstacles. Managing the assimilation process is especially difficult where the cultures and control systems of the merging firms are very different.

We agree that these challenges and resultant failures are to be found on a significant scale, and they form part of our explanation. But we find them an incomplete explanation of the ever-increasing volume of M&A in the face of ever-increasing evidence of adverse impacts on performance. M&A attracts some of the brightest graduates from the universities—to work on merger within acquiring businesses or in the M&A departments of investment banks, consultancies, legal firms, etc. And a great deal of experience has been accumulated on the challenges of M&A and effective responses to meet them (e.g. Galpin and Herndon 2014, and Fernandes 2019). So it is puzzling that capable executives—supported by talented and highly-trained advisers and monitored by profit-seeking shareholders—having observed or experienced so many failed mergers, would double down on acquisition activity, to lead a forty-fold increase over forty years.

This is the core of the mystery, and the puzzle seems too deep to be explained away merely as the 'triumph of hope over experience'.[18]

What Counts as Success or Failure in Merger?

Table 1.1 presents a stylised income statement (profit and loss account) that provides a framework for our discussion of the mystery. It follows the pattern familiar to anyone who reads business accounts: money in and money out. Column A gives a benchmark for assessing the success or failure of a merger: what the income statement would look like if the two merger participants had remained independent and their two separate statements were simply added together. It shows first the revenue coming into two merging firms, and the costs of operating the firms. Revenue minus costs gives operating profit (or loss). This tends to be what concerns the industrial economist. The statement then shows the profit which has to be paid in interest to those who have lent to the firm, and next the corporation tax payable on post-interest profit. 'Earnings' are the residual—what's left for shareholders. This can be paid out to shareholders as dividends or ploughed back into the business to generate future dividends, and is typically a measure the financial economist will focus on in assessing M&A 'success'.

Table 1.1 Stylised income statements of merging firms

Column A	Column B
A benchmark: the sum of the participants' income statements if they had remained independent	**The income statement of the merged firm**
REVENUE	**REVENUE** *Plus any higher revenue from better products* *Plus any higher revenue from monopolistic pricing*

---

18   Reported by Boswell (1791) as Dr. Johnson's comment on a man's second marriage.

Column A	Column B
Minus **COSTS**	Minus **COSTS**
	Plus any (net) synergies
	Minus increased executive pay
	Minus merger transaction costs
Equals **OPERATING PROFITS**	Equals **OPERATING PROFITS**
Minus **INTEREST**	Minus **INTEREST**
	Plus any gains from extra borrowing
Minus **TAX**	Minus **TAX**
	Plus extra tax subsidies
Equals **EARNINGS**	Equals **EARNINGS**
	(as in Column A, plus *net merger benefits to shareholders*)
	Loss of consumer surplus harms the customer, but not the business

From the shareholders' perspective, a merger is successful if it leads to higher earnings. This is if the post-merger earnings are accurately recorded—a big 'if' in the case of merger, as Chapter 9 explains: merger offers rich opportunities to flatter earnings through creative accounting.

The potential sources of gain from merger for the shareholder are inserted in italics into the statement in Column B. The revenue of the combined firm might be increased—without, or net of, associated cost changes—if the merger results in improved products which command higher prices. For example, one firm might bring design skills which enhance the other's products. Other things equal, this is a win for the shareholders, and it's a win for the wider economy—better products, a social gain.

However, the shareholders would also win if revenue rose and earnings swelled because monopoly power was increased by the merger. For example, the only two airlines operating on a particular route (with exclusive landing rights) could raise fares once competition was eliminated in a merger. But the passengers would lose. The profits which come at the expense of those customers who continue to fly but pay more are recorded in the income statement. But there is an extra cost borne by those who are priced out of the market. This latter 'consumer surplus' problem is of course the focus of much of the work of antitrust/ competition authorities. If the competitive fare before merger was $100, and the monopoly price afterwards was $150, passengers who would have been willing to pay, say, $125 lose out. There is a loss of allocative efficiency—they lose access to a service which could be provided for $100 and is worth $125 to them.

This loss of consumer surplus will not appear in the merged firm's accounts. So a merger which shows improved profit feeding through to earnings for shareholders in the accounts may be a failure on a social calculation because it has deprived customers of benefits. Chapter 2 gives examples of pharmaceutical companies hiking prices after merger—e.g. serial acquirer Valeant raised the price of its diabetes drug, Glumetza, from $572 to $5,148 (Tepper and Hearn 2019, p. 168). With demand for this treatment remaining high ('inelastic' in economist's terminology), the supplier's income statement would be likely to show startling success. Patients dependent on the treatment and priced out of the market might take a different view.

The next part of the income statement—costs—can again offer the prospect of synergies and closer alignment of private and public benefit in merger. This is where evidence would appear after merger of the scale economies associated with Adam Smith's division of labour, or Neutron Jack's or Fred the Shred's slashing of costs in the acquired business. Such cost reductions[19] would feed through to shareholders' earnings.[20] They would also release resources for use elsewhere in the economy—a potential national gain (though the supplier whose margin is in jeopardy, or the worker who is fired, may not see it that way).

Two new costs are generally found in the accounts of a merged firm which would not have arisen if the two firms had remained independent: additional pay for the acquirer's senior executives (commonly) and fees to professional advisers (always). In relation to the massive scale of some firms participating in merger, these expenses may seem scarcely to be material—even at the top end, tens of millions for the executives and a billion or so for the advisers are dwarfed by firm size. But for the recipients of these substantial personal payments they can of course

---

19 Net of cost changes resulting from any diseconomies of scale.
20 There could be further earnings gains if the opportunity to reduce prices led to a substantial boost in sales.

be highly material, and distort the incentives they face. They may lead to deals which are successful for executives and advisers but not for shareholders or the economy at large. Chapters 2 and 3 explain.

The next two lines of the income statement are: interest and tax. We explain in Chapters 5, 6 and 7 how these appropriations can change in the course of merger, with 'subsidies' enjoyed by shareholders of acquiring firms—as borrowers and taxpayers—at the expense of other groups in the economy. These privileges can result in earnings gains—success— for the shareholders in mergers even where the combinations yield no gains, even declines, in operating profits. If the buyer's capital structure could be modified in merger, by borrowing on favourable terms to buy the target's shares, the acquirer's shareholders could secure the target's post-interest profit for no outlay of their own money. Benefits would also accrue to the acquirer's shareholders if the merger succeeded in reducing the tax payable on the combination's profits.

This accounting framework is suggesting then that promoters of merger are sometimes right that a deal offers the prospects of success both for the shareholders and for the economy at large: it can be positive-sum, with private and social interests coinciding. However, the framework indicates too that merger can offer a quick, legal and easy way of achieving success for the shareholder at the expense of other interest groups (zero- or negative-sum). Of course, the economics of monopoly are well understood by policymakers: eliminating competitors via merger can bring success for shareholders at the expense of customers and suppliers. But there are also other zero- or negative-sum routes to success for shareholders that are less prominent in the literature. Limited liability for shareholders allows them to 'privatise [the] gains and socialize [the] losses', as Fleischer (2020) puts it, associated with a debt-financed merger. And tax systems offer a range of privileges to merging firms.

Many of the studies of the effect of merger on performance employ earnings measures, or stock market measures heavily influenced by earnings measures. But these are typically an upwardly biased proxy for operating profits because of the opportunities offered by merger for tax avoidance and gains at others' expense from borrowing. And operating profits are themselves typically an upwardly biased proxy for the social gains from merger when revenue and costs benefit at customers' and suppliers' expense because of increased market power.[21] So if even earnings-based measures turn out to be no better than neutral on the gains from merger, this is likely to be bad news for the economy at large.

Appendix 1 discusses further these performance measures and, as mentioned above, reports over 50 studies which have measured operating profit, or earnings, or share price appreciation during and/ or following merger. Despite so many potential sources of gain for the shareholders, and on the face of it curiously, the statistical evidence on post-merger earnings does indeed show that often even the acquirer's shareholders fail to gain from increased earnings or share prices.

Plan of the Book

Section A of Part Two below discusses the benefits for prime-movers of M&A—senior executives of the acquirer, and advisers—even where the merger leads to falls in operating profits. These two groups are often faced with incentives to undertake mergers which do not serve the interests of their principals—the owners (shareholders) of the acquirer. A merger is typically a financial success for the executives who lead it (Chapter 2). And a merger deal is almost always financially successful for the advisers (Chapter 3), even if it is adverse for the rest of the economy.

Section B of Part Two then describes some of the financial engineering which can make mergers attractive to shareholders even when they lead to a decline in operating profits. In this case, the action takes place in Column B of the income statement in Table 1.1. Chapter 5 discusses the lure of debt-financed merger: limited liability provisions for the borrower skew the borrower's calculations—much of the burden of downside risk is shifted to other interest groups, while the full upside benefit accrues to the borrower. The benefits of debt-financed acquisition do not end there: they are magnified by the privileged treatment of interest payments under most current tax regimes (see Chapter 6). And even where mergers are not debt-financed, in most jurisdictions they offer target shareholders the opportunity to convert 'income' into 'capital gains' which enjoy privileged tax treatment. Finally, cross-border mergers

---

21 Reported profits will also be an upwardly biased proxy for operating gains if the acquirer takes advantage of the rich opportunities afforded by merger for creative accounting designed to inflate the profits reported by the amalgamation (Chapter 9).

with companies headquartered in jurisdictions with low tax rates on profits can sometimes be used to reduce the acquirer's tax bill. Chapter 7 describes some of the most sophisticated financial engineering—practised by private equity funds.

Section C of Part Two, 'Information Asymmetry', concerns the information available to investors on the performance and prospects of merging firms. Share prices in imperfect markets deviate from the prospective earnings they are supposed to reflect; and this creates opportunities for acquirers to make speculative gains from deals which do not augment (even lower) operating profits. Creative accounting by bidders ahead of an offer can magnify information asymmetries between executives and shareholders and facilitate mergers which are not in the latter's interests. Accounting for the deal itself provides rich opportunities to flatter post-merger profits (and conceal post-merger losses). And conventions for accounting in post-merger years can allow executives to misrepresent the outcome of deals.

Part Three of the book, 'Review and Reform', first pulls the strands of the book together by charting the experience of two acquiring businesses which combined many of the problems identified in earlier chapters. It then outlines potential ways of eliminating or at least mitigating those problems.

PART TWO

DETECTION: FOLLOWING THE CLUES

Section A

Misaligned Incentives for Executives, Advisers and Others

'Show me the incentive and I will show you the outcome', observed Charlie Munger, Vice Chairman of Berkshire Hathaway.[1]

This section explores incentives facing key M&A participants which can contribute to the mysterious and puzzlingly persistent outcomes of zero or negative operating gains. It discusses participants who initiate, support or approve M&A: the acquirer's executives and NEDs (non-executive directors), their professional advisers, and the representatives of the target's shareholders.

---

1   Quoted in Edgecliffe-Johnson (2021).

2. Incentives for Executives

Even in mergers where bidding shareholders are worse off, bidding CEOs are better off three quarters of the time. (Harford and LI 2007)

The prime movers in M&A are the senior executives of the bidder, especially the CEO and CFO. Their formal role is to pursue the interests of their principals, the shareholders. Yet their shareholders have often lost out from M&A. We need to explain why executives may proceed with deals that do not serve the interests of their shareholders, let alone their other stakeholders or the economy in general. We begin by exploring the incentives facing senior executives, focusing on the consequences of M&A for their pay, perks, power, protection, and prestige.

Pay

We use the shorthand term 'pay' for all the monetary benefits paid to executives. The typical package for a CEO in Western companies comprises base salary, which doesn't vary with profits or share price, and short-, medium- and long-term bonus schemes which relate payments to the achievement of performance targets, payments which sometimes come in the form of shares or share options.

In determining base salary, remuneration committees often hire remuneration consultants, who provide benchmarks such as the average paid to executives of similar firms (plus a bit, of course, for the 'Lake Wobegon Effect'—everyone in the fictional town being convinced they were better than average). One key 'similarity' is company size: the taller the pyramid of managers—the more layers of management in an organisation—the higher the pay of the boss tends to be. Statistical studies have found a strong correlation between firm size and the pay of the top managers, independent of performance (e.g. Meeks and

© 2022 Geoff Meeks and J. Gay Meeks, CC BY-NC-ND 4.0 https://doi.org/10.11647/OBP.0309.02

Whittington 1975; Blanes et al. 2019). So expanding the size of your firm is one way of securing a pay rise.

How to achieve rapid expansion? Hargreaves (2019, p. 47) reports that the average British CEO is in office for five years, 'so if they want to make their mark, along with their fortune, they need to get a move on.' Just keeping pace with the growth of the market will often not produce much growth and rise in pay in those five years. For instance, in Western countries from 2014–2019, if you managed to expand sufficiently to maintain your market share, and the market was growing in line with the GDP of the countries you supply, your business might typically grow by perhaps 2% a year.[2] Growing by M&A instead is seen as much easier than increasing market share or developing new markets.[3] The $27 billion acquisition of Refinitiv by London Stock Exchange Group (LSE) in 2021 tripled the acquirer's revenue in a month (Elder 2021b). The Chief Executive was 'rewarded with a 25 per cent increase in base salary [...] to reflect the LSE's increased size following the Refinitiv purchase' (Stafford 2021). Stafford notes that in the same month, LSE shares fell 25%—on concerns about 'LSE's ability to extract synergies from its acquisition of Refinitiv'.

Of course, expanding size to justify a bigger salary may well bring no benefits to the wider economy. Executives and commentators sometimes speak of growth of the firm as if it equates with growth of the economy, and brings corresponding social benefits, such as more output, more capital assets, or a greater range of products and services. But there is a fallacy of composition here:[4] the growth of a firm by M&A can mean just a reallocation of share ownership, with no change to the size of the economy. Promoters of M&A are, of course, only too pleased to conflate the two—expansion of the economy on the one hand and reallocation of ownership of a part of the economy on the other. And they don't mention the resources that are consumed just to achieve a reallocation of share ownership: the substantial transaction costs of a merger deal, which we illustrate in the next chapter.

---

2   The average annual growth rate of GDP in constant prices for all OECD countries for 2014–2019 was 2.2% (OECD.Stat).
3   Kay in Kynaston (2001, p. 748).
4   The error of assuming that what is true for the member of the group (the firm) is true for the group as a whole (the economy). On economic growth itself, see the qualifications in note 8 of this chapter.

From the perspective of the economy, some critics would describe merger not as 'growth' but as corporate 'cannibalism'. Similarly, the critics sometimes describe the acquisition of a domestic firm by a foreign one not as direct 'inward investment', but as 'the sale of the family silver'. In neither case does the acquisition in itself expand the productive capacity of the economy.

In the last three decades, although executive pay is still correlated with firm size and growth, increased emphasis has been placed on better aligning managers' interests with those of shareholders through performance-related pay (PRP). Jensen and Murphy (1990) were among the academics calling for this development after noting that:

> Public disapproval of high rewards seems to have truncated the upper tail of the earnings distribution of corporate executives [...] The resulting general absence of management incentives in [...] corporations presents a challenge for social scientists and compensation practitioners. (p. 227)

Among the businesses responding enthusiastically to this 'challenge' was Enron, for several years named 'America's Most Innovative Company' by *Fortune* magazine, and itself the product of a merger and the initiator of significant M&A deals. Enron's experience gives a hint of potential problems with PRP. Performance-related benefits were important in swelling the compensation of its senior executives to $845 million (over $150 million to the chairman alone) in the year ending in its bankruptcy (Ayres 2002).

The *Financial Times* Lex column (2017) analysed the role of PRP in a specific large acquisition by Reckitt Benckiser (RB)—of Mead Johnson. A performance-related pay scheme for the Reckitt Benckiser CEO included 'a yearly award of shares through "long-term incentive plans". These pay out in proportion to growth in earnings per share (EPS).' Lex reported that the debt-financed acquisition was estimated to result in extra EPS growth for Reckitt Benckiser of 7%, 12% and 16% in the years 2017, 2018 and 2019. And the consequent payouts from the incentive plan would sum to around $15–17 mn.

Now at first sight this arrangement—targeting and rewarding EPS—appears to be an efficient way of aligning the interests of the CEO with those of the shareholders: more earnings per share for the owners brings more 'pay' for the CEO. But a problem arises which, in other economics contexts goes under the name 'Goodhart's Law'.[5] In essence, this says, 'When a useful measure becomes a target, it ceases to be a good measure'. In the context of M&A, those who stand to benefit from reaching a target may look for ways of appearing to achieve the performance target without genuinely improving underlying performance (or, worse, while delivering weaker underlying performance); and in the case of M&A, there are powerful means for doing that. In Chapters 9 and 10 we explore devices associated with M&A accounting which boost reported EPS without any improvement in underlying operating profits (even despite a deterioration). In Chapters 5, 6, and 7 we investigate the way that financial engineering with M&A may do the same (especially in a debt-financed deal), again delivering higher EPS while operating profits are unchanged or diminished. In Ford's (2020) words:

> Existing contracts that are poorly designed allow bosses of quoted companies to become rich by using leverage to game earnings per share and performance targets.

In extreme cases the required 'performance' has simply been to make the acquisition: the acquirer's boss has been directly rewarded just for pulling off what proved to be an unfortunate deal, without having to show change in a targeted performance measure. Hargreaves (2019, p. 79) cites the case of Vodafone's acquisition in 2000 of

> Mannesmann for $181billion—[at the time] the largest corporate deal in history—its boss [...] received a special pay deal of $10million to reflect the success [in completing the deal]. However the merger went badly wrong and is now taught as a case study in business schools as one of the most value-destroying takeovers in the corporate world. (p. 79)

Vodafone wrote off some $43 billion of its purchased goodwill in 2006, mostly in relation to its purchase of Mannesmann (Amel-Zadeh et al. 2016).

In that same deal, it was alleged that the executives of the acquiree also benefitted very directly from the acquisition. Mannesman's CEO and five other directors were taken to court by shareholders, accused

---

5   The 'law' was developed in the 1980s when the British government used the supply of money as the policy target in the attempt to control inflation. The former strong correlation between money supply and inflation broke down: inflation accelerated despite tight control of the money supply.

of having received excessive payouts by Vodafone to give up resistance to the deal (*Guardian* 2004).[6] Sweeteners for the acquiree's executives featured also in the Reckitt Benckiser case: the *FT*'s Lex concluded that the CEO of Mead Johnson, the target, 'should get an [...] impressive $13.7m pay-off if he steps down, as expected'.

The pattern of benefits to the acquiree's executives in these examples is not exceptional. In a statistical study, Hartzell et al. (2004) found that executives in the acquired business often gain significant financial benefit from M&A, and those gaining particularly generously have tended to agree lower acquisition premia for their shareholders. The misalignment of incentives identified by Harford and Li (our quote at the head of this chapter)—bidding executives gaining even where shareholders lose out—can therefore sometimes be seen in the acquiree too.

Perks: Benefits in Kind

Greater size often means a bigger geographical spread of subsidiary companies for the boss to monitor, and the associated luxury travel is a welcome perk for some: glamorous hotels and private jets become 'essential'. The CEO of serial acquirer GE, Jeffrey Immelt, travelled in one private (company-funded) jet, and this was followed by a second GE private jet (Muolo 2017). The purpose of the second jet is unclear; but rumour has it that in one other notorious case a second jet carried a CEO's pet dog. Again, as with pay, if M&A delivers a large increase in size, the CEO's peer group changes, and this affects the accepted norms for benefits. Hargreaves (2019) quotes Warren Buffett: 'CEO perks at one company are quickly copied elsewhere. "All the other kids have one"' (p. 48).

Given such packages of financial incentives it is hardly surprising that senior executives avidly seek out acquisitions even where they promise little or no gain in operating performance. But this is not all: there are other powerful incentives to do deals which benefit neither shareholders nor the wider economy. These are to do with power, security and prestige.

---

6   The court decided that their actions did not constitute wrong-doing.

Power and Protection

Writers on the role of merger in industrial organisation and public policy have given most attention to the effect of merger on market power: increased prices charged to consumers and reduced prices paid to suppliers (including labour) once competitors are eliminated. We gave a striking illustration for the US aviation industry in Chapter 1. Detailed statistical and case evidence on various industries is provided by Philippon (2019) and by Tepper and Hearn (2019). Part of the mystery we are addressing is the puzzle of why—given the opportunities for merging firms to secure more favourable prices—we don't see more evidence of gains in operating profit for the merging companies. And part of the solution is that the benefit from increased market power *may* take the form not of higher profits for shareholders, but of enhanced power and protection for the acquirer's executives.

In elaborating the theory of monopoly, Nobel Laureate John Hicks (1935) commented: 'the best of all monopoly profits is a quiet life' (p. 8). Subsequent writers developed the argument. For example, Leibenstein (1966) argued that in circumstances where pressure from competitors is light, many managers will opt for less effort and search, and enjoy the utility of feeling less pressure. Then Cyert and March (1963) predicted that, other things equal, the costs of firms that hold dominant positions in the market will tend to rise.

Wu (2018) describes Facebook's use of M&A to secure a 'quieter life'—to stifle competitive threats and protect high profits. Instagram 'gained 30 million users in just eighteen months of existence [...] was poised to become a leading challenger to Facebook based on its strength on mobile platforms, where Facebook was weak [...] Facebook realized it could just buy out the new [competitor]. For just $1billion, Facebook eliminated its existential problem...' (p. 122). And then 'Facebook was able to swallow its next greatest challenger, WhatsApp, which offered a more privacy-protective and messaging-centered competitive threat' in a $19billion buyout...' (p. 123). 'In total, Facebook managed to string together 67 unchallenged acquisitions', consolidating its monopoly power.

Similarly, Philippon cites a study of predatory acquisitions in the pharmaceutical industry, where incumbents have been found to pre-empt future competition by acquiring a firm which is developing a product which would rival its own, and shelving the innovative competitor: 'A large incumbent may want to acquire a target and shelve its products. Cunningham, C., Ederer, F., and Song Ma (2018) call this a "killer acquisition" [...] A drug project is less likely to be developed when it overlaps with the acquirer's portfolio of existing products'(p. 82).

As well as protecting executives from pressure in the markets for the acquirer's output and inputs, M&A can also reduce the pressure in the 'market for corporate control'—pressure arising (as Chapter 1 noted) from the threat of being taken over oneself, perhaps putting their own executive positions at risk if performance flags. In an early statistical study for a substantial set of firms, Singh (1975) found evidence that 'as a survival strategy, attempting to increase relative profitability may well be inferior to attempting to increase relative size, particularly for larger unprofitable firms'(p. 510). Consistent with this, Meeks and Whittington (2021) show that, with just one exception (Tesco—a 'minnow' in 1948), it has only been very large firms that have survived long periods without being acquired. Bayer paid $63 billion for Monsanto in 2018 'because this promised to make the chemicals group invulnerable to takeover' (Guthrie 2020). From a shareholder's perspective this deal, according to one analyst (Bender 2019), 'ranks as one of the worst corporate deals in recent memory': Bayer's share price fell by over 40% in the year after deal completion.

Another use of surpluses resulting from the elimination of competitors is to gather political support to protect the executives' privileged position (with the access of large corporations to political power that the Harvard economist Galbraith (1967) had begun to observe in the 1960s). The means by which influence is secured vary from country to country: it may include hiring lobbyists, funding politicians, and creating revolving doors between government and business (Meeks, Meeks and Meeks forthcoming). And the influence can be deployed to resist more stringent competition policies, and gain government contracts, as well as to protect the distorted accounting, morally hazardous legal arrangements, and privileged tax codes which we discuss in later chapters.

Prestige

In professional sport, the prestige of different teams is typically reflected in their performance ranking in leagues. And those rankings are of course based on success measures such as number of wins, and goals or points or runs scored. In business, the rankings are very often based on measures of size. This is rather as if football league rankings were to be based on the size of the respective clubs' stadiums.[7] Media admiration of Neutron Jack (Welch) typically highlighted his creation of the *biggest* corporation in the world: he was a celebrity, best-selling author, management guru. Fred the Shred took special pleasure in building the *biggest* bank in the world; and as noted in Chapter 1 he joined distinguished figures such as Nobel Laureates and military and sporting heroes in being knighted by the Queen.

Sometimes the more sophisticated media use a rather more dynamic metric when ranking businesses. For example, the *FT* publishes rankings by revenue growth (FT 2021). And at first sight this seems congruent with the still most widely used indicator of national economic advance (though one that is flawed as a measure of gain in well-being),[8] the

---

7   For example, the *Fortune* 500 is a league table ranked by revenues; so are Statista's Top 100 Companies: UK and Top 100 Companies: USA; and also 'Top 100 Companies in the World' published by corporateinformation.com.
     Some, such as *Forbes* Global 2000, combine pure size measures (assets, sales) with ones reflecting performance (market value, profits); but still a merger boosting size but not performance would advance a business in the league table.

8   As the European Commission (2022) puts it, 'Economic indicators such as GDP were never designed to be comprehensive measures of prosperity and well-being'. Though representing countries' levels of production (subject to qualifications concerning depreciation, unpaid work and so on), GDP data fall seriously short if (mistakenly) held to reflect economic welfare—neglecting, for instance, negative externalities such as environmental degradation (Pigou 1920; Mishan 1967) or distributional issues affecting health and educational outcomes (Sen 1999): in Sen's words, 'without ignoring the importance of economic growth, we must look well beyond it [... for] an adequate conception of development' (p. 14). Principles of well-being—which have a very long pedigree—have gained increased policy prominence in recent decades, with Bhutan's preference since 1972 for its GNH (Gross National Happiness) measure, the UNDP's establishment of the HDI (Human Development Index) in the 1990s; the European Commission's 'Beyond GDP' initiative launched in 2007; the Commission on the Measurement of Economic Performance and Social Progress's Report in 2009 (Stiglitz, Sen and Fitoussi), with follow-up work continuing, supported by the OECD; the UN supported World Happiness Reports from 2012 onwards (Helliwell, Layard and Sachs 2012); and, from the UK Treasury, the Dasgupta (2021) Review. This caveat is relevant also

growth of GDP. But as we suggested earlier, the analogy between business growth and GDP growth is seriously misleading in the presence of M&A. M&A in itself does not expand the production or incomes of an economy: the deal simply reallocates control over an existing bundle of assets. And it consumes resources in the process—the transaction costs we discuss in the next chapter. Yet in spite of this, growth by M&A is widely admired, much as a spurt in GDP growth is standardly taken to add lustre to the reputation of a country's president or prime minister.

The *FT's* Collins (2014) captures the attraction for the CEO:

> Think of the impact of a 'transformational' deal, the thrill of the chase, the media spotlight, the boasting rights and—of course—the massive pay rises. You will be number one! [...] By the time it all ends in tears, the executives who have laid waste to the shareholders are long departed with their winnings. [...]
>
> So when the investment bankers send round their hottest M&A boys, the executives are vulnerable to a sales pitch.

In the next chapter we report on why 'the investment bankers send round their hottest M&A boys'—the incentives facing these investment bankers and other professional advisers on M&A.

---

to the post-merger economic performance measures discussed in Chapter 1 and Appendix 1.

3. Incentives for Advisers

Probably the single most important word in the corporate finance business is 'no'—when said to a client to explain why his deal will not work and cannot be backed. But it is a word which can cost a firm clients since it is one which thrusting entrepreneurs and captains of industry are not accustomed to hearing. (Terry Smith 1996)

The Scale of Advisers' Fees in M&A Transactions

Table 3.1 summarises the fees and other transaction costs incurred in the merger of Belgian ABInbev and South African SABMiller to form a dominant international brewing combination with 170,000 employees. The total M&A transaction costs for the two businesses were around $2 billion (2.5% of deal value); but part of this was Stamp Duty (transaction tax), so professional fees summed to about $1.5 billion, some 1.9% of deal value. Towards half a billion of this was spent on advice from banks and management consultants; three-quarters of a billion for arranging the borrowing used to finance the deal. The rest went to lawyers, PR consultants and accountants. The outcome of the deal has not impressed commentators who have studied the merged firm's financial performance.[1]

A similar pattern was reported for the £24.3 billion purchase in 2016 of Arm Holdings by SoftBank: £96 million (about 0.5% of deal value) to banks for their advice to the two businesses ('for a few weeks' work,' according to Vincent 2016a), and another 0.5% for arranging borrowing.[2]

---

[1] Massoudi and Abboud (2019) report that three years after the deal, ABInbev's shares 'sit 26 per cent below the level they were at in October 2016 [...] The world's biggest brewer is still carrying $106 billion of debt taken on to pay for the deal' — with businesses being sold off 'to chip away at the debt'.

[2] We recognise that fees for deals which go ahead have to be set at a level sufficient to cover the adviser's other activities and expenses such as negotiations with potential clients which do not lead to engagement.

© 2022 Geoff Meeks and J. Gay Meeks, CC BY-NC-ND 4.0 https://doi.org/10.11647/OBP.0309.03

In 2020 advisers were brought in again as SoftBank proposed to sell Arm to the US firm Nvidia in order to reduce its borrowings.[3]

Table 3.1

Transaction costs: ABInbev/SAB Miller merger

$ million	ABInbev	lead firm	SABMiller	lead firm
Financial & broking	135	Lazard	113	Robey
Fees for raising debt	725			
Legal	185	Freshfields	76	Linklaters
PR	20	Brunswick	9	Finsbury
Accounting, etc.	15		4	
Management con-sultancy, etc.	180			
Other costs				
Stamp duty	475	HMRC		

Source: Massoudi, A. (2016) 'ABInBev-SABMiller deal to yield $2bn in fees and taxes', *FT*, 27.8.16.

As we have recognised above, in a sector characterised by huge numbers, such as finance, it can be hard to take in numbers ending in so many zeros. A yardstick can help. Collins (2019) provided one for the aborted bid by Sainsburys for Asda. If a deal is aborted the transaction costs are typically much smaller as a proportion of the deal value—an important point in our discussion below of conflicts of interest. Nevertheless, as Collins (2019) pointed out, they were the equivalent of 'the margin on £2.3billion of sales', which gives a sense of the time and effort required 'as the (mostly poorly paid) staff in Sainsbury's supermarkets try to generate sales to pay the fees'.

Another useful yardstick is to compare the sums derived from this work by the advisers' employees with average incomes. Just as with the executives in the previous chapter, performance-related pay is an

---

3   The proposed deal was abandoned in February 2022 in the face of opposition from competition authorities.

important component of the employees' incomes: staff bonuses are related to getting the deal done and to the fees so generated. The banks supplying such advice offer rich rewards to their staff in M&A. In the US and the UK, the most active centres of M&A transactions, rookies start with pay three or four times the median annual salaries of the whole national workforce. Senior staff ('managing directors') are eligible for very large bonuses related to the fees they earn for the bank, and their pay can reach three hundred times the national median pay.[4]

If deals do go ahead, the feeling of wellbeing does sometimes 'trickle down'. Vincent (2016b) notes: 'When five Barclays bankers dined out on a deal in 2002, they paid 500 per cent over the odds for three bottles of Petrus, a Montrachet and an Yquem. Plus two pints of lager. Their waiters split £5,500. Nice work if you can get it.'

The Dilemma for the Adviser

Put yourself in the position of the investment banker earning your living through M&A advice. Suppose the executives are eager to go ahead with a deal—for some of the diverse reasons outlined in the previous chapter. But in the light of your knowledge of the two businesses and the sector and the market conditions, you have serious doubts about the gains to be had by shareholders from the proposed merger. How vigorously do you try to persuade your client to abandon her aspiration to expand her business in this way? If she does give up, you can only claim reimbursement for the staff time and expenses in compiling the advice ('only' as represented in the Sainsbury's example above). But if the deal goes ahead, payment will typically be in the form of a substantial success fee calculated as a percentage of the deal value. Moreover, there will also often be lucrative fees to be won for organizing the funding of the deal. Clearly, the adviser's direct financial interest is generally served by the deal going ahead, not by it being aborted.

There is also a relationship to safeguard. If the client executive's longer-term strategy is to grow by M&A, do you want to lose the opportunity to build the relationship while completing the deal, and to secure a favoured position when advisers are being arranged for the

---

4   https://corporatefinanceinstitute.com; https://mergersandacquisitions.com; https://arkesden.com; https://www.statista.com; https://ons.gov.uk.

next M&A deal or other banking services? Under CEO Jack Welch, GE was on average completing about four deals a month over the final two decades of last century (Gryta and Mann 2020, p. 17). His successor continued the M&A strategy. Crooks (2018) reports on the fees earned from the acquisition programme of GE since 2000:

> The dealmaking was great for GE's advisers. Banks that worked with GE on its deals, including Goldman Sachs, JP Morgan and Morgan Stanley, earned hundreds of millions of dollars for their advice since 2000, data from Thomson Reuters show. Coupled with the work Wall Street offered underwriting debt, equity and loans for the group, GE proved a critical client. Since the turn of the century, it has paid more than $6bn in fees, according to the data provider.

The incentive for bank advisers not to deter potential acquirers from going ahead is reinforced by the way 'success' is measured by the media. Just as the kudos of business executives is reinforced by rankings based on the size of the business rather than its profitability (Chapter 2), so also the rankings for M&A advisers are based on the fee income secured by the banks.[5] Completing the deal brings not only the immediate financial benefit, but also the glamour of heading, or rising in, the fee rankings. And that in turn raises your visibility to would-be acquirers looking for an adviser to drive through a deal.

A Surprising Insight into How Much Work Expert Advisers Sometimes Do on a Deal

The interaction between M&A advisers and acquirer executives takes place behind closed doors. But aspects of that relationship were revealed for the RBS/ABN AMRO case by a UK Parliamentary Committee (HoC 2012). The acquirer failed during the financial crash 12 months after this deal was completed, and received a 45-billion-pound government bailout. The parliamentarians—in the case of this excerpt from the transcript, Jesse Norman—were exploring the case with distinguished financiers, including Sir David Walker, whom the committee had asked to review the case on their behalf:

---

5   E.g. ig.ft.com/wall-street-fees. Some use another scale measure (to which fees are closely related)—deal value: mergermarket.com, dialogic, and *WSJ*.

Extract from a transcript of part of a meeting of the House of Commons Treasury Committee discussing the failure of RBS (HC640)

January 24, 2012

Q83 Jesse Norman: Yes, thank you. Did you see the report from the advisers that they would have given to the directors?

Sir David Walker: There was certainly one major report. At the time when the board were first considering the ABN AMRO acquisition possibility, which was probably about February/March—I don't know the precise date and my recollection is not clear—there was a report, the thrust of which was supportive of this being an attractive opportunity, something like that.

Q84 Jesse Norman: That report would have modelled the financial effects of the takeover?

Sir David Walker: No, I don't think it did. I don't think that question had been posed. I think the question that was posed was, "Here is an opportunity. Is it interesting for us?" It was at a fairly high level I recollect.

Jesse Norman: But there must have been some projection of the financial benefits. The board must have had some advice as to what the financial implications of buying an institution worth €71 billion were, for its own balance sheet, for its own liquidity, for the status of its own operations.

Bill Knight: I am sure they did. You should bear in mind, of course, that €71 billion was the total price. RBS's share of that was 38%.

Jesse Norman: Yes, it was about €27 billion.

Bill Knight: Yes, that is right, so it was actually much smaller.

Jesse Norman: But the board was, nevertheless, buying into a transaction of the larger size and one would have expected that the portions it was buying would have been in substance modelled pro forma into its own P&L, into its own financial statements, into its own capital requirements.

Sir David Walker: My belief is that although they had that advice at the beginning, which was generic, rather high level advice—saying, "This is an interesting opportunity to pursue"—most of the arithmetic, the pro forma stuff of the kind you refer to, was done within RBS in the ensuing period, and the focus of the adviser was in the execution of the transaction, not advice on the way it could be done.

Q85 Jesse Norman: Does that mean that the adviser never actually gave the advice that what you might call a traditional financial adviser would give, "Is this a good transaction for you"?

Sir David Walker: It depends what you mean by "traditional financial adviser". I think the error of omission there, and it is what leads us to make a specific policy proposition, is that in situations of this kind if it were to happen again it should be the norm that independent advice is taken, which is not remunerated on the basis of success with the transaction.

Jesse Norman: That is what I am trying to get at.

Sir David Walker: Yes.

Q86 Jesse Norman: A final question: how would you assess the quality of—

Chair: A very quick question and a very brief answer.

Jesse Norman: Very quickly, but it is rather germane. Did you have a chance to assess the quality of due diligence that would have been given on the purchase by the advisers?

Sir David Walker: No.

Jesse Norman: Or indirectly come to a judgment on it?

Bill Knight: The due diligence done by RBS was inadequate.

Chair: Was?

Bill Knight: Inadequate. There is no doubt about that.

Jesse Norman: Could you just describe it a little bit more so we can get a sense, don't forget we haven't seen any of it and we would like to know just how inadequate it is, the kinds of things it covered or did not cover.

Bill Knight: It was famously, in April at least, two lever-arch files and a CD. That is what is referred to in the—a very minimal amount of information was given, so it was largely based on published information, the reports to the board. The PWC report [...] clearly concludes that this was inadequate.

Q87 Jesse Norman: So the punch line is that the transaction of €27 billion was made by the board without independent financial advice on the back of thoroughly inadequate due diligence by Merrill Lynch for which they, and other advisers, would have been paid well north of €100 million or €200 million. That is the punch line of what you are saying?

This excerpt relates, no doubt, to an extreme case; but it is revealing in three respects. First, it is consistent with other evidence on the remarkable scale of fees paid to M&A advisers for apparently modest amounts of work (we noted above that £96 million were paid in the acquisition of Arm Holdings 'for a few weeks' work'). The advisers would hardly be unhappy if the deal went ahead and this fee could be claimed. Second, the advisers were seemingly not expected to, and did not, complete a thorough analysis of the prospects for the deal.[6] And third, the independent members of the RBS board, representing shareholders, had not sought independent advice on the merits of this proposed expenditure of €27 billion of shareholders' money, RBS's share of the deal. We return to the role of non-executives on the board in the next chapter.

The Revised Sequence

They think up deals and egg you on, so they can make a fat profit
Joe Hyman, Chairman of Viyella International. (Kynaston 2001, p. 373)

The language of investment banking conjures up an image of a potential acquirer identifying a target and then seeking the services of professional advisers—banks, lawyers and other professionals—to advise on and then implement the strategy which the potential bidder has devised. This is the 'accepted sequence' of textbook market economics: businesses respond to the autonomous demands of their customers. But in his 1966 Reith Lectures, Galbraith had proposed an alternative concept— the 'revised sequence' whereby powerful businesses actively devised products and used their sophisticated marketing operations to persuade customers to buy them (Galbraith 1967). The revised sequence accounts for part of the M&A market.

An historic US example of a banker actively promoting merger is provided by JP Morgan, who, early in the twentieth century, famously initiated mergers to combine the three major steel producers into US Steel, so that it controlled 70% of US steel production (Tepper and Hearn

---

6   Currently, companies listed in the UK are required to provide detailed financial information in (Class 1) cases where the acquisition is large relative to the acquirer's size. This would be compiled by the investment bank adviser, but responsibility for the underlying financial data would rest with management.

2019). His other amalgamation initiatives included the formation of Northern Securities Company, which dominated the railroad industry. In the UK, the revised sequence was firmly established forty years ago. Kynaston (2001, p. 605) describes the approach of the 'hot competitive force in the takeover field'—Morgan Grenfell: '[...] in the corporate finance department, where from 1979 there was a systematic policy of targeting companies that could potentially be persuaded into launching a takeover bid.' England and Kerr (2020) describe the same approach by bankers—of pitching potential cheap takeover targets to investors who had spare cash—during the COVID 19 crisis. 'We are presenting every opportunity we can to the Gulf and Singapore', a London-based banker said, 'They are all going to get great deals right now'.

We were reminded of this by experience with one of our very bright graduate students. He took a year out from the M&A department of an investment bank to pursue one of our Master's programmes. One of the courses he joined was in financial reporting. The course had been built around a very detailed analysis of the latest accounts of a single listed company. One of us had invested a lot of time in background research on this business and the quirks and puzzles in the accounts of this specimen firm.

After the course the student returned to his investment bank. In no time at all, even before the next year's cohort of students had got to grips with our case company's latest accounts, news came that the company was being taken over. It emerged that the adviser to the acquirer was the employer of our former student. We later discovered that his first project on returning to the bank had been pitching our case company to a client as an attractive means of expansion.

From the teaching point of view, this unfortunately meant going back to the drawing board to create a fresh new course around a different company, hoping that none of the class would repeat this process.

Special Purpose Acquisition Companies (SPACs)

The revised sequence has in recent years been taken to a new level by the use of SPACs—special purpose acquisition vehicles. Whereas in the original revised sequence the financial institution identifies an existing company to pitch to another company as a potential acquisition—to generate fees from the transaction—a SPAC is a shell company which lists on a stock exchange, raises money for an acquisition, and then searches for a private company to buy, bringing it onto the stock exchange.

Wolf (2021b) paints an unflattering picture of SPACs:

> These are vehicles for the acquisition of unlisted companies and so a way around initial public offering rules. They are modern versions on a vastly bigger scale of the company allegedly created during the early 18th century's South Sea bubble, 'for carrying on an undertaking of great advantage, but nobody to know what it is'. That bubble ended badly. Will this time be different?

In the US, SPACs raised over $55 bn in 2020 (Aliaj, Indap and Kruppa 2020); but volumes were much lower in the UK (Hodgson 2020).

Aliaj et al. report that typically the sponsors of the SPAC begin with a 20% stake in its equity, costing just $25k. Their share diminishes when an acquisition is undertaken. But one investment banker sold part of his original $25k stake for $60 million. And Aliaj et al. quote the hedge fund leader Bill Ackman describing the SPAC structure as 'one of the greatest gigs ever for the sponsor'. Because of the favourable purchase of equity at a discount by the sponsor(s), the sponsors can still gain even when the acquired business falls in value. The *Financial Times* reported that the majority of SPACs organised between 2015 and 2019 were trading below the price at which they had been listed (Tett 2020).

Other Perks for the Advice Industry

A participant in one of our finance courses came up at the end of a class and said, 'I've paid a lot of money to come on this programme, and I expect a handsome pay-off. How can I use the material in the course to recoup my fees? I don't care whether the scheme is legal, provided that I can be sure of getting away with it.'

We declined to answer. But one answer could have been 'the ever-vexed area of frequently perpetrated, infrequently prosecuted insider dealing, still the classic white-collar crime' (Kynaston 2001, pp. 775–76). In the M&A field, special opportunities arise in relation to the premium typically offered to target shareholders. If you bought shares in the prospective target when a deal was first seriously mooted, and sold them at the time of the deal, you might make a return of, say, 30% over a few months. Who has the information to make those trades? One group includes the professional advisers who prepare the campaign, documentation, etc. before the deal is announced. This is not to suggest that professional advisers in general lack integrity. But the path of the typical target's share price in the weeks up to announcement of the deal is consistent with some insiders taking advantage of this opportunity.[7]

The regulators (in the UK, the Financial Conduct Authority) are wise to this: 'suspicious trades occurred before 30 per cent of takeover announcements in the UK in 2009 according to FCA statistics' (Binham 2016, p. 18). Binham gives examples: a group of City professionals were alleged to have made insider trading profits on acquisitions including that of Scottish and Newcastle by Carlsberg and Heineken (£4.4 mn in profit) and Ncipher by Thales (a profit of £724,000). Two of the group were convicted and jailed.

FT Reporters (2016) had fun with a pun, when relating a case of information 'leakage' to a plumber ahead of M&A: 'A former Barclays director [Mr McClatchey] stands accused by US prosecutors of allegedly committing insider trading to pay for home improvements', by passing inside information on upcoming mergers to his friend, who was a plumber.

> The plumber, Gary Pusey, has pleaded guilty and agreed to cooperate with authorities.
>
> The government alleges that Mr McClatchey, who worked in a back office role, gave tips to Mr Pusey, 47, ahead of at least 10 separate transactions before they became public, including deals involving Petsmart, CVS and Duke Energy.
>
> In exchange for the tips, which allegedly earned Mr Pusey $76,000 in trading profits, the plumber made cash payments totaling thousands of dollars to Mr McClatchey by occasionally placing cash in a gym bag or handing the cash over directly to Mr McClatchey's garage, it is alleged.
>
> He also provided a free refitting of Mr McClatchey's bathroom...

Some economists have argued that insider dealing is an efficient method of keeping markets informed of the true value of a firm's shares when a potential acquisition was in the offing but had not been announced. The counter-argument, associated particularly with Nobel Laureate George

---

7   Though it is unlikely that the prime movers in M&A, such as CEO or lead advisers, would take part.

Akerlof (1970), is that if the market is rigged to benefit insiders, outsiders will be deterred from investing and the economy will be deprived of the risk-sharing, liquidity and other benefits of large markets.

For a long time, insider dealing was not seen as an offence in the UK, and was considered a legitimate perk for people working in the financial markets. As Kynaston reports (p. 594): 'in June 1980—at long last— insider dealing became a criminal offence, though few were holding their breath that any such criminals would be put behind bars.' But monitoring by regulators and by employers has continually increased, so that the risk of detection and punishment will have deterred some would-be dealers.

If there are adviser-insiders who have invested in target shares, their gain will be maximised if the deal goes through, selling when the shares reach their peak. The prospect of a lucrative premium is realised on completion of M&A. For an inside trader, whether or not the deal will produce operating gains does not matter.

But similarly, the legitimate opportunities M&A generates for the community of bankers and other professional advisers are very lucrative, whatever the outcome for shareholders and other stakeholders.

In 1940 Fred Schwed wrote a classic book on financial investment with a telling title. In it he tells the story of 'an out-of-town visitor being shown the wonders of the New York financial district. When the party arrived at the Battery, one of his guides indicated some handsome ships riding at anchor. He said, "Look, those are bankers' and brokers' yachts."

"Where are the customers' yachts?" asked the naive visitor—the words Fred used as his book's title. Endorsing the reissued book in the twenty-first century, Michael Bloomberg commented, 'The more things change the more they stay the same.'[8]

---

8   In the 2006 edition.

4. Incentives for Other Participants

One newcomer to the board under Welch was surprised by the CEO's command of the board room and the sparse debate among the group. Confused by how the meeting transpired, the new director asked a more senior colleague afterward, 'What is the role of a GE board member?'
'Applause,' the older director answered. (Gryta and Mann 2020, p. 21)

Non-executive Directors

In mergers of smaller businesses, the owner-manager of the acquirer would typically agree a deal with the owner-manager of the target. But in the mergers of larger, listed businesses, on which this book concentrates, there is of course typically a 'divorce' of ownership and control, and the owners of the acquirer and the managers of the target may play only a limited role. The two leading decision-makers in a deal are the acquirer's CEO and the target's shareholders. The former has to persuade the latter to trade their shares for the acquirer's shares, or for cash.

The acquirer's CEO will spend a good deal of time in conclave with her adviser from the investment bank, who will sometimes have identified the target and suggested the acquisition in the first place (see Chapter 3). The target's shareholders will receive advice from the target's board, and, particularly if it is an offer of the bidder's shares in exchange, rather than of cash, will receive information from the acquirer's CEO on the acquirer's record and the prospects for the combined company. Much of this information will have been prepared by advisers in the pay of the acquirer, on the basis of information provided by management.

© 2022 Geoff Meeks and J. Gay Meeks, CC BY-NC-ND 4.0   https://doi.org/10.11647/OBP.0309.04

As we show in later chapters, the most consistent winners from merger are these three groups: the acquirer's CEO,[1] the acquirer's investment bank and other advisers, and the target's shareholders.

The acquirer's shareholders, on the other hand, have a much smaller role, despite the fact that they will be seriously affected by the terms of the deal and the combination's performance after the merger. Sometimes—for example if the deal requires a large increase in share capital—they may get a vote. And if they cannot challenge the proposal by 'voice'—a vote—they can 'exit': sell their shares. If this occurs on a significant scale it may lead to a fall in share price. And if shares are the currency of the offer, target shareholders may be deterred from accepting. For example, when Couche-Tard bid for Carrefour in 2021, while the target's shares rose by 13%, the bidder's shares fell 10% (Abboud 2021). And the bid was abandoned (Abboud and Kirby 2021).

One other potential channel through which acquirer shareholders might influence the merger decision is through the group of (part-time) non-executive directors (NEDs) on the acquirer's board. They are expected to represent the interests of shareholders. But there is anecdotal evidence that their scrutiny is weak (see the quote at the head of this chapter, and Chapter 11). And—paralleling Chapter 3's discussion of financial advisers—put yourself in their position: is it in their interest to challenge—to make trouble for—a CEO who is set on an acquisition? NEDs of UK FTSE 100 companies were typically paid in the order of £100,000 for their very part-time job in 2020 (four times the average full-time wage in Britain) (Deloitte 2021). Gaining a reputation as a troublemaker who challenges the CEO might not help retain this role or garner other lucrative part-time non-executive positions: around two thirds of those already making 100k (on average) held at least one other directorship (Hargreaves 2019).[2]

Fund Managers

In many cases, the executives of the bidder do not need to get the approval of their shareholders for an acquisition.[3] Mostly the only influence of the

---

1   And other internal partners of a private equity fund (see Chapter 7).
2   This is not to say that every NED will be driven by self-interested motivation.
3   Listing Rules for the UK Stock Exchange do require a vote by the acquirer's shareholders where target size exceeds a given proportion of the acquirer's size.

acquirer's shareholders on the outcome is through the 'exit' option of selling their shares in the bidder. In a cash bid the acquirer's executives can ignore this; only in a share for share bid might exit affect the outcome (as in the Couche-Tard bid). It is the target's shareholders who reliably have a direct role—'voice'—in the process: the requisite majority must accept the offer if the deal is to proceed.

In practice, the choice of the target shareholder will mostly be exercised not by the person who has invested in the share, but by an intermediary such as a fund manager acting for a pension fund or insurance company.[4] Where does her interest lie? Again, as in the case of the acquirer's CEO and the acquirer's professional adviser, the pay and promotion of pension fund managers is typically linked to performance. And performance is often measured by the quarterly change in the value of the manager's fund.

The bidder typically has to offer the target shareholder a premium over the pre-bid price of the share on the market. This is because the pre-bid price is that which induces the marginal buyer and the marginal seller to trade, and some shareholders, believing the prospects of the target firm are worth more than the pre-bid price, will only sell if they receive at least that higher valuation. The typical premium required to secure control—to persuade enough intra-marginal holders to part with their shares—averages around 30% (Amel-Zadeh and Meeks 2019). If the deal goes through, this is the wealth gain for the marginal shareholder in the target; but for all intra-marginal shareholders, the gain is smaller, and for the last shareholder to agree, very small—had the premium been 1% less, she would not have sold.

But for the fund manager, her portfolio records an immediate gain on the target's shares of the full 30%. And performance-related benefits linked to the fund value will rise correspondingly. She may therefore be willing to sell for a lower premium than those she acts for would require for themselves. Kynaston (2001, p. 673) quotes a fund manager weighing up a bid: "'I will probably accept the Hanson Paper [Hanson shares offered in exchange for United Biscuits shares] because I cannot afford to miss out on short-term performance of shares'".

And Somerset-Webb (2017) illustrates the misalignment of incentives:

---

4   Institutional ownership in the FTSE 100 was reported as 62% by Segerstrom (2020).

Take mergers and acquisitions. If you are a fund manager holding an investment that attracts a bid at a 40 per cent premium, you'll vote to take it. Can't be bad for the performance numbers on which your bonus is based, can it? But is that what the pensioner, who was enjoying the steady growth in the dividend yield from the same investment, is also likely to do?

Pointing out that short-termism in investment is a problem is not exactly new...

Academic Experts

The acquirers sometimes call at universities, tempting academic experts to lend enthusiastic support to the promoters of a deal. Here, once again, financial incentives tend to be aligned with the acquirer's interests. An academic colleague who was expert on M&A once explained to us that, when a merger was being investigated—and possibly blocked— by the regulator, the pay he would be offered for an hour's work on the promoter's side was roughly equal to that for working a day on the (government) regulator's side. As before, put yourself in his position... But, being public-spirited and content with an economical lifestyle, he resisted these inducements and chose not to work for the highest bidder.

Section B

Distorted Financial Engineering: Moral Hazard, Tax Privileges and Private Equity

The previous section focused on the role of misaligned incentives in zero- or negative-sum mergers. In some cases executives found that their private interest lay in mergers which turned out to yield zero or negative gains for their principals, the shareholders. Representatives of shareholders—variously non-executive directors and fund managers—sometimes found their private interest lay in acquiescing in, or supporting, such mergers. So did advisers to bidding firms.

In this section we explore additional motives for zero- or negative-sum mergers, where the losers may not be shareholders but other groups with an interest in the business—especially creditors, employees, pensioners, taxpayers, and lenders. These are cases in which shareholders do not necessarily lose out if operating profits decline, and may acquiesce in a merger which yields operating losses. Executives may still be giving priority to their private interests, but gains at the expense of other groups may compensate shareholders. These other groups may be disadvantaged as a result of legal, taxation, and central banking arrangements, which often bring benefits both to shareholders and to executives whose pay (Chapter 2) is linked to earnings or share prices.

Chapter 5 discusses moral hazard—the incentive to take on more risk because you don't carry the full cost of that risk. It explains that limited liability provisions in law allow acquirers to restrict their risk to what is often a modest equity stake, with the necessary remaining finance provided through taking on debt. If external shocks don't eliminate the slender equity cushion, the equity-holders' earnings are typically magnified by the reliance on debt. But if the slight equity cushion is exhausted by such shocks, the losers often include employees, former employees, and unsecured creditors.

Chapter 6 reports on arrangements that are in effect subsidies to acquirers from government. Heavy reliance on debt is further encouraged by privileged treatment in many tax systems: corporation tax is not levied on the portion of profits paid out in interest. A substantial debt-financed merger can therefore reduce the overall tax payable by the combination. Then, recently, 'asymmetric monetary policy' has reinforced the privileges accorded by the tax system: since the 2008 financial crisis, central banks, seeking to support the economy, have manipulated the market for debt so as to hold down interest rates payable by borrowers.

Chapter 6 discusses two other tax privileges which provide motives for acquisitions that bring zero or negative operating gains. These are not directly related to debt-financed M&A, though they often accompany highly leveraged acquisitions (especially in the Private Equity model outlined in Chapter 7). First, mergers can convert income streams into capital gains, which have enjoyed favoured tax rates. Second, cross-border mergers have been used as a method of international tax arbitrage—shifting the acquirer's profits to a lower tax regime.

Whereas many of the characteristics of M&A advisers, stock markets, and accounting systems highlighted in other chapters are common to most jurisdictions, there is more diversity across the world in the legal, taxation and regulatory regimes we discuss in the next three chapters. Most of our illustrations are for the UK and the US—historically the most active M&A markets.

5. Moral Hazard

[...] the Fed estimates that corporate debt has risen from $3.3tn before the financial crisis to $6.5tn last year.

Much of this debt has financed mergers and acquisitions and stock buybacks. [...] they boost earnings per share by shrinking the company's equity capital and thus inflate performance related pay. Yet this financial engineering is a recipe for systematically weakening balance sheets. (Plender 2020)

Excessive leverage is the juice that enables businesses to privatize gains and socialize losses. (Fleischer 2020)

Magnifying Earnings with Debt Finance

The arithmetic of inflating performance-related pay by raising gearing with a debt-financed merger is simple, and we doubt whether many readers need any explanation. Just as putting a vehicle into a higher gear leads to more revolutions of the wheels for given revolutions of the engine, so higher gearing of the business typically leads to more earnings per share (EPS) for given operating profits.

As in Chapter 3, we draw on the case of Belgium-based AB Inbev's 2016 acquisition of fellow beer business, South Africa-based SAB—here to illustrate the arithmetic of debt-funded acquisition. The deal gave the merged firm control of over 2,000 beers and a powerful position in the US and other markets.[1] Their respective financial statements show that before the acquisition AB Inbev, the acquirer, had a gearing ratio, g (the ratio of borrowing to the sum of equity and borrowing), of 0.5 (rounded); for the target, SAB Miller, the ratio was roughly 0.3. But after the acquisition was completed, the ratio for the combined business had risen to 0.6, the deal having been supported partly by a syndicated loan

---

1   Tepper and Hearn, p. 188; Wu, p. 117.

© 2022 Geoff Meeks and J. Gay Meeks, CC BY-NC-ND 4.0   https://doi.org/10.11647/OBP.0309.05

of \$75 billion. As the two firms enjoyed returns on net assets[2] before the deal exceeding 10%, and were able to borrow at around 3% (SAB Miller 2016, p. 4), this increased indebtedness is likely to have enhanced the return on equity,[3] and earnings per share (EPS), albeit at the cost of increased risk. The improvement comes from borrowing money at 3% and investing it at, say, 10%,[4] without there needing to be any improvement in the operating profit generated by the firm's assets. EPS could increase even if operating profits declined. We noted in Chapter 3 the disappointing financial outcome of this merger.

Limited Liability and Moral Hazard

Other things equal, the smaller the equity cushion, the higher are EPS. But this 'weakens balance sheets': the business is less able to weather losses in adverse conditions (e.g. a pandemic) and avoid insolvency. However, limited liability (the norm for businesses) reduces the downside for shareholders and strengthens the incentive to take on borrowing: it means that if the business fails, the most the shareholders can lose is their own stake in the balance sheet (their initial subscription of equity plus any earnings retained by the business on their behalf). If the firm becomes balance-sheet insolvent (their assets are less than their liabilities—'negative equity'), the equity shortfall hits other stakeholders in the business: lenders and others owed money by the business will not get all they are owed. There is 'moral hazard'—the borrower shifts some of the downside costs of risk-taking and so has an incentive to take on extra risk for the sake of potential gain.

Contrast this privilege with the typical UK home-buyer's unlimited liability when she combines her funds (a deposit—her equity) with a mortgage from the bank. If she has to sell the house and its value has fallen below the mortgage outstanding (she has 'negative equity') she has to make good the deficit: unlike equity-holders in a limited liability company, her obligation is not limited to the equity she committed.

---

2   Earnings before interest and taxation (operating profits), divided by (the sum of equity and non-current liabilities).
3   Earnings after interest and tax, divided by equity.
4   Where the buyer pays more than book value for the target (the usual situation), the return on the newly acquired assets will of course be less than 10%.

The slender equity stakes contributed by acquirers in some deals is illustrated by Walmart's sale of Asda, their top-4 supermarket chain in the UK, at a valuation of £6.8 bn. Smith and Wiggins (2021) reported that 'The private equity backed billionaires buying Asda will pay less than £800m of their own money to take a controlling stake in the supermarket...' The rest was funded by borrowing, and by the proceeds of selling Asda assets and leasing them back. Their equity stake was just 12% of the purchase price, whereas 'on average, European leveraged buyouts had an equity contribution of more than 50% in 2020'.

Inevitably, smaller cushions of equity heighten the risk of failure. In analysing the eventual closure of Debenhams, the major UK department store chain founded in 1778 and operating 118 stores, Elder (2021a) discusses the role of the owners' 'over-enthusiastic cash-extraction' in earlier years. He recalls that:

> CVC, Texas Pacific and Merrill Lynch acquired Debenhams in 2003 in a 1.8bn pound leveraged buyout that needed just 600m of equity. The trio then extracted more than 1bn via property sale and leaseback arrangements and floated it [on the Stock Exchange] again for nearly the same price in 2006.

The earlier extraction of cash had left the business with diminished equity—reserves available to meet setbacks.

We discuss below some of the losers from the limited liability of borrowers. Professional lenders such as banks aim to protect themselves by demanding a premium in the interest rate that they charge—to compensate for the risk arising from the limited liability of the borrower. Also, they typically demand security—a first claim on certain assets of the borrower in the event of failure. And they incorporate covenants in their contracts, allowing them to intervene if performance flags— for example if interest cover (profit/interest) falls below a defined threshold.[5] However, the incidental 'lenders' we discuss below (trade creditors, members of a company pension scheme), are less able than banks to protect themselves from the consequences of limited liability. And this can lead to severe problems of 'moral hazard'. Some experts

---

5   Though the rich opportunities to flatter reported profits after merger via creative accounting (Chapter 9) can subvert this last safeguard in the case of M&A.

in this field have proposed that the limited liability of some corporate borrowers ought to be restricted (Goodhart and Lastra 2020).

Free Loans from Suppliers

Carillion offers a striking example of free 'loans' from suppliers as a funding source, documented in a UK Parliamentary Committee Report (HoC 2018). It grew through a series of mergers into one of the largest UK construction companies, operating in several countries. The monopsonistic power Carillion had achieved—partly though acquiring rivals—allowed it in effect to demand from its suppliers interest-free funding. As it turned out, this carried very high risk. Suppliers were pressed to agree to payment for their goods and services as late as 120 days from delivery, even though Carillion had joined the UK Government's Prompt Payments Code which targeted payment within 30 days, and stipulated that 95% be paid within 60 days (HoC, p. 40). This arrangement obviously increased the amount Carillion owed to suppliers at any one time. And when Carillion failed (in 2017–2018) it owed around £2 billion to 30,000 suppliers, who would receive little from the liquidators, and some of whom were themselves bankrupted as a result. Carillion is analysed in detail in Chapter 11.

Free Loans from Pensioners

Members of companies' defined benefit pension schemes have sometimes unwittingly financed acquisitions of the companies for which they work. And they have in some cases suffered significant losses as a result, when the acquiring company went on to fail. The key features of such a process are illustrated by an acquisition documented in detail in another UK Parliamentary Committee Report (HoC 2016). Dominic Chappell's RAL (Retail Acquisitions Limited) acquired Sir Philip Green's retail chain, BHS (British Home Stores)—all the assets of this old-established national store chain—its properties, equipment, inventory, brand, etc.

How much did RAL pay? One pound. How come?

Sir Philip was a shrewd and very successful businessman, not someone you would expect to give away a retail empire for next to nothing. A key part of the answer lies in the defined benefit pension fund for BHS employees. Such funds—now shunned by most private sector employers—arose from past contracts with employees to pay a defined pension throughout their retirement (Meeks 2017). The pensions were part of the remuneration packages—deferred pay—offered by employers. Year by year employers (and employees) paid contributions to a pension fund designed to meet these pension obligations. But BHS had failed to accumulate assets in its pension funds sufficient to meet its prospective pension obligations. When Sir Philip bought BHS in 2000, the pension fund's assets exceeded its prospective obligations by £43 million; when he sold it in 2015, there was a shortfall on some estimates of £350 million.

When Mr Chappell bought BHS in 2015, he took ownership of the company for a pound; but his company also assumed liability for these pension obligations. It was analogous with assuming responsibility for a loan to BHS from a bank, with this loan funding the entire operation—without any equity stake from the 'owners'. In effect, there was no material equity in the business. In the year following the acquisition Mr Chappell, who 'had a record of bankruptcy [...] and neither retail experience nor any experience of running a similar-sized company' (HoC 2016), oversaw a further decline in operating performance at BHS (the common post-merger pattern we documented in Chapter 1). Yet Mr Chappell's company extracted £11 million in fees from its BHS subsidiary and £6 million in loans, while he personally took £2.6 million in salary and fees (a pattern of executive behaviour familiar from Chapter 2) and an interest-free loan of £1.5 million, which was not repaid. In 2016, not long after Mr Chappell's purchase, BHS went into administration. 11,000 employees lost their jobs; and 20,000 current and former employees faced major cuts in their pensions: on one calculation, the pension fund deficit by then totalled as much as £571 million. The HoC Report encapsulates the moral hazard in this high-risk acquisition: 'The tragedy is that those who have lost out are the ordinary employees and pensioners'. In the end, Sir Philip Green, the vendor of the business, yielded to huge political and media pressure and paid £363 million into the pension fund—'likely to help the billionaire keep his knighthood' (Ruddick and Butler 2017); and the average employee lost 'only' 12% of her pension benefits.

This was an extreme version of moral hazard in funding an acquisition. The acquirer made in effect a one-way bet: if it came off, he won all the future earnings of BHS; if it didn't, he just lost his pound but the current and former employees lost some of their pensions.[6]

---

6   This is in addition to the adverse impact on employees' mental health of the acquisition process itself. Bach et al. (2021) provide statistical evidence of the mental health effects; Hill (2019, 2022) gives specific examples.

6. Subsidies for Merging Firms

Eliminating the corporate interest deduction would reduce the incentive to borrow excessively. (Fleischer 2020)

[…] tax free capital gains—these, among other factors, fuelled the coming of the takeover bid. (Kynaston p. 63)

A cross-border takeover is to Britain's tax lawyers and accountants what a well-fed wildebeest with a limp is to a pride of lions. And this one, the meatiest one ever to have lumbered across the savannah, would be devoured more greedily than any before or since. From the moment the takeover was conceived, 'tax planners' from City law firm Linklaters and accountants PwC were set to work. (Brooks 2013, p. 95, on Vodafone's $180 bn acquisition of Mannesmann)

[…] the central bank has, in some profound way, manipulated the market. (Foroohar 2022)

These four quotes relate to different subsidies available to businesses which have made acquisitions. The subsidies are discussed in turn in this chapter. First comes the tax break which has been extended to interest on debt used to fund M&A. Second is the way in which promoters of merger have been allowed to convert 'income' into more lightly taxed 'capital gains'. Thirdly, some cross-border acquisitions have enabled acquirers to reduce the combination's tax bill. And lastly we turn to manipulation of interest rates by central banks, which has had the incidental effect of favouring debt-financed acquisitions.

Subsidising Corporate Debt Used to Fund Merger: Tax-deductible Interest

In most jurisdictions, corporation taxes are levied on the portion of profits due to shareholders but not on the portion paid as interest to

© 2022 Geoff Meeks and J. Gay Meeks, CC BY-NC-ND 4.0 https://doi.org/10.11647/OBP.0309.06

bondholders—it is puzzling as to why. We have tried to find a persuasive case for this tax break, but failed. In contrast there are compelling arguments that it promotes excessive risk-taking, and should be eliminated.[1] In the meantime, this privileged treatment of interest on borrowing inevitably makes it even easier to transform poor profits into enhanced surpluses for investors via a debt-financed merger.

Brooks (2013) gives revealing illustrations. He reports Spire, acquirer of BUPA hospitals, 'wiping out its taxable profits by paying interest offshore at 10%' (p. 141). And in the case of Thames Water, acquired (with a roundabout structure) by Macquarie, he links 'tax-deductible interest costs, most of it on debt owed to the offshore investors' to the result that 'in the two years to March 2011, from a £1.2bn operating profit the group that own Thames Water paid UK corporation tax of £19m' (p. 211).

Using Merger to Convert Income into More Lightly Taxed Capital Gains

Tax systems vary greatly between countries and over time. But one feature which has been fairly common, and which provides incentives for M&A even where there are no operating improvements to be had, is privileged tax status for capital gains relative to 'income'. An extreme version of this was evident in the UK in the period after the Second World War. Tax rates on personal income (including dividends) were at historically high levels; but capital gains were untaxed. This affected the decisions of shareholders in M&A targets on whether to accept a bid offer with tax-free capital gains, or to reject the offer, in favour of retaining the rights to heavily taxed future dividends from the target. Kynaston (2001) writes:

> [...] reduced dividend payouts to shareholders as a result of increased company taxation since the war, and the natural appeal to shareholders of tax free capital gains—these, among other factors, fuelled the coming of the takeover bid. (p. 63)

---

1   E.g. Armstrong (2020), Ford (2020b), Vandevelde (2020).

In the UK (and US) today, capital gains are taxed, but at privileged rates. And one of the fields of activity where the disparity has attracted particular criticism is the private equity (PE) industry. The business model of PE companies has been characterised as 'buy out businesses, load them with debt, and sell them' (Wade 2020).[2] They are leading players in M&A: they 'struck deals worth \$559 bn worldwide in 2020 [...] More than 8,000 deals were announced [that] year, the most since records began in 1980' (Wiggins 2020b).

Early in this development Brooks (2013, p. 160) explains that the leading players 'made their serious income by putting in a small amount of their own money, typically between 1% and 3% of the investment in a fund, in return for perhaps 20% of the fund's profit. Treated as a capital gain on an investment, this so called "carried interest" would be taxed at a quarter of the top income tax rate...' Chapter 7 explores the Private Equity model in more detail.

International Tax Arbitrage via M&A

When you are teaching an MBA class in which there are almost as many nationalities as students, you soon realise how hard it is to generalise about tax arrangements across jurisdictions. Differences between countries are in some cases not accidental, but jealously preserved, with countries using preferential tax deals to attract multinationals to locate activities there. Sandbu (2021) cites estimates that 40% of global foreign direct "investment" [including M&A] is structured to lower taxes rather than for actual business investment reasons.

Such differences between countries in tax rates on businesses can then create incentives for M&A which have no other commercial logic. Tax rates on some parts of the profits of corporations headquartered in the US have sometimes been significantly higher than the rates in other jurisdictions. Simply redomiciling the business to take advantage of a lower tax regime was not allowed. But merger with a business in the lower tax jurisdiction could enable the combination to pay the lower tax rate. Americans for Tax Justice claimed that US Burger King's acquisition

---

2   'When you've got the Fed saying debt will stay cheap for years [...] the numbers look buoyant', said Bryce Klempner, partner at consultant McKinsey (quoted in Wiggins 2020b).

of Canadian Tim Hortons and redomiciling of the group in Canada could save some \$275 m in US taxes from 2015 to 2018 (Drawbaugh 2014). The pharmaceuticals giant Pfizer sought by M&A to qualify for a lower tax rate by moving its tax base from the US to the UK or Ireland. Such a "tax inversion" motive was explicitly linked to Pfizer's bid for AstraZeneca in 2014 and for Allergan in 2015 (Crow and Ward 2016).

We quoted above Brooks' colourful description of the tax avoidance opportunities afforded by UK Vodafone's acquisition of German Mannesmann. He reported that 'This was serious "tax efficiency", wiping hundreds of millions of pounds every year off the company's tax bill.' (Brooks, p. 100)

The gain at the expense of national finances was then very significant even if the deal delivered no operating gains. As it turned out, the deal yielded disappointing operating results, and £23.5 billion of the investment in Mannesmann was written off in 2006. (Amel-Zadeh, Meeks and Meeks 2016).

Annexe to Chapter 6

Subsidising Corporate Debt: Monetary Policy Reinforcing Tax Policy

In the wake of the 2008 financial crisis, central banks wisely adopted ultra-loose monetary policy, resulting in substantial reductions in interest rates—of the order of 2%.[3] Without the intervention, the financial system was in danger of collapse. The intervention was expected to be short-lived. However, for various reasons the authorities found it convenient to continue rigging interest rates. Politicians have been fearful of restoring interest rates to their level before central bank intervention: this would increase the cost of servicing government debt and be likely to result in (politically unpopular) lower prices for assets such as houses and company shares. There developed an '"asymmetric monetary policy", whereby they supported markets when they plunged but failed to damp them when they were prone to bubbles. Excessive risk-taking in banking was the natural consequence' (Plender 2020).

Rigging the market gave some borrowers an 'exorbitant privilege' (Acharya et al. 2022): the debt was in effect subsidised by the lenders, including individuals with savings accounts or those buying annuities for retirement, for whom lower interest rates mean reduced incomes. The global stock of non-financial corporate bonds doubled in real terms between 2008 and 2019 to $13.5 trillion (Plender 2020). Among the beneficiaries were merging companies: the subsidy further magnified the gain in earnings which could be reported after a debt-funded merger which yielded no operating gains. Debt-finance came to overtake share exchange as the preferred funding mechanism for M&A. Commenting on the study from the Federal Reserve Bank of New York authored by Acharya et al. (2022), Lex (2022) wrote: 'The trillions they were able to raise at alluringly low rates were often ploughed into M&A [...] These dealmaking sprees turned out to be disastrous for those companies...'

---

3   See, e.g., BT (2010).

7. Private Equity (PE)

> Private equity is all about risk. Funds are notorious for allowing their portfolio companies only a slim financial cushion to ride out economic downturns [...]
>
> There have been many examples of funds risking a thin sliver of their own money as equity, providing the rest of the finance their companies need with debt and then walking away from investments that go wrong. Many have paid themselves big dividends from increased debt [...] Pension funds and others often pay high fees for what they are told is better management on behalf of the industry. (*FT Leader* 2020a)

Serial acquisition such as the conglomerate GE had practised has in recent years been increasingly supplanted by private equity (PE) firms. GE— which acquired around a thousand businesses in the last two decades of the twentieth century—has more recently been divesting businesses and finally breaking itself up into specialist firms. But private equity funds have been expanding their activities. There were nearly 7,000 private equity firms in the US in 2019. Even in Europe, they have accounted for almost 40% of M&A volumes recently, over half of those deals in the UK. Their individual scale is illustrated by one of the pioneers of the PE industry, KKR, which has bought some 400 companies since its foundation in 1978, at a cost of $650 bn; and its portfolio of companies employs over 800,000 people (Vandevelde 2021).

At first sight a PE business looks like a traditional conglomerate. But there are some significant differences. For example, PE businesses generally run funds with a limited life: their acquisitions are reorganised and sold after a few years, the proceeds distributed to the subscribers. Conglomerate acquirer GE, by contrast, was a continuous member of the Dow Jones Industrial Index from 1886 to 2018 (Dissanaike et al. 2022). Then, whereas GE has generally been headed by an industrialist promoted from within the company, KKR was led by three former

© 2022 Geoff Meeks and J. Gay Meeks, CC BY-NC-ND 4.0 https://doi.org/10.11647/OBP.0309.07

employees of the investment bank Bear Stearns. And the typical business model of PE executives has differed from the traditional conglomerate in the way they have managed acquired businesses, in their use of financial engineering, and in their incentive schemes for the top management.

Managing Acquired Businesses

One source of gain sought by PE has been to mitigate the principal-agent (or 'stewardship', or 'governance') problem associated with public companies run by salaried managers and owned by dispersed, remote shareholders. Concentrating ownership in the PE fund removed the free-rider problem in a public company, where, with large numbers of shareholders, individual shareholders would devote limited effort to monitoring and disciplining management when most of the benefits went to others. And the PE arrangement mitigated some of the information problems to be discussed in Chapter 9: shareholders in public companies are only entitled to the information mandated by law and the regulators, while the PE firm could demand whatever information they deemed necessary to monitor and guide the acquired business.

And then, the individual acquired companies in the PE portfolio have been funded with very high levels of borrowing, designed to strengthen incentives to generate profit and not to dissipate it in ways discussed in Chapter 2. This debt creation '[...] enables managers [of the acquired businesses] to effectively bond their promise to payout future cash flows' (Jensen 1986). If they failed to meet the interest and principal payments they would end up in bankruptcy court. And, in Jensen's words: 'These transactions are creating a new organizational form that competes successfully with the open corporate form because of advantages in controlling the agency costs of free cash flow' (p. 325).

Financial Engineering

As well as sharpening the incentives facing managers of the acquired businesses, heavy reliance on debt funding could bring additional benefits discussed in Chapters 5 and 6: magnifying the returns to equity holders, securing tax breaks, and taking advantage of the government distortion of interest rates after the financial crisis. The increase in reliance on debt funding has been dramatic: 'financial debt of non-financial US firms [not just PE] has grown 30-fold in the past 50 years...' (*FT Leader* 2021). Chapter 5 reported on a recent acquisition in the UK—of food retailer Asda—where the equity subscribed by the buyers (the Issa brothers and PE fund TDR Capital) totalled just £780 million of the purchase price of £6.8 billion. (Lex 2021)

Chapter 5 discussed the benefits to equity-holders of limiting their stake in the business, outlining the arithmetic of debt finance—the attractions of borrowing at, say, 3% to buy assets yielding 10%. If the business performs well, earnings for equity are inflated by heavier reliance on debt finance. If it performs poorly, limited liability provisions mean that equity-holders lose only their stake. Other interest groups (sometimes unwittingly) can bear most of the downside costs. Ford (2019) provides an illustration:

> Toys R Us, the US retailer [...] fell into liquidation last year after more than a decade of private equity ownership [...]
>
> Investors lost the slender equity stakes they had contributed [...] But it was far worse for the workforce. Tens of thousands not only lost their jobs, but their entitlement to severance pay as well.
>
> The private equity firms later made a $20m payment into a workers' hardship fund to try to quell the ensuing rumpus (staff representatives claimed they were owed $75m). But that just served to highlight the disparity between what the buyout bosses felt they owed and what they had extracted. Over the 12 years of the buyout, they had banked riskless management fees of $470m.
>
> Toys R Us is far from the only example of this sort of 'heads I win, tails you lose' capitalism.

As Chapter 5 discussed, borrowing brings the further benefit that the interest payments are typically deductible in the calculation of corporation tax. Then, since the financial crash of 2008, the opportunities for financial engineering have been further reinforced by central banks' interventions to force interest rates below the level they would reach in a free market. Wiggins (2020b) commented: 'The US Federal Reserve's decisions to cut interest rates to zero [...] ensured private equity's continued access to cheap debt for new deals [...] "Ultimately the lifeblood of private equity is cheap debt", said Bryce Klempner, partner at consultant McKinsey.' A later comment reinforced the point: 'They all think they're geniuses because their companies are doing really well', quoted Wiggins from one commentator, who went on: 'But if it weren't for central bank policy, things would be very different' (Wiggins 2021).

Easy access to debt has meant that the PE owners could extract large sums of cash without first making profit in their acquired companies. Rennison (2020) gives the example of snack foods maker Shearer's Foods, owned by Chicago-based PE company Wind Point Partners and the Ontario Teachers' Pension Plan: 'It raised more than $1billion in the loan market on Tuesday, in part to fund a $388m payment to its owners, according to ratings agency Moody's.'

The importance of the financial engineering motives for PE acquisitions, rather than stimulating stronger operating performance in the acquired business, can be inferred from commentary on the acquisition of the UK food retailer Morrisons by Clayton Dubilier and Rice, the US private equity group. The acquirer's adviser, Terry Leahy (a leading expert on the industry), described Morrisons as already 'an excellent business with a strong management team, a clear strategy and good prospects'. And Eley (2021) reports that 'Analysts have questioned how any owner will be able to generate a return on such an outlay on Morrisons without big asset disposals.'

Incentives for Top PE Executives

Chapter 2 focused on the misalignment of incentives facing the top executives of traditional (non-PE) acquiring businesses. Many benefits accrue to those executives whether or not an acquisition enhances operating performance; and efforts to link their pay to performance have been criticised as too weak (Jensen and Murphy 1990), or because they were too easily subverted by creative accounting—or indeed by distorted financial engineering. The PE industry has responded to these challenges by linking investment managers' benefits more securely to those of the external investors, redesigning the system of incentives and making them much more powerful. The PE firms may manage a number of PE funds, each with several investments in their portfolio. The funds buy and sell businesses, and are typically liquidated after around five to seven years. The PE firms receive management fees of up to 2% of the funds' assets. In addition they receive a performance fee—up to 20% of the fund profits[1]—a very direct alignment of interest.

As mentioned in Chapter 6, the benefits for the PE managers are further enhanced by another tax privilege. The profits (confusingly called 'carried interest', or 'carry' for short) are taxed at lower rates than, say, salary. Philippon (2019) reports that in the US, carry qualified for a capital gains tax rate of 23.8% rather than an ordinary income tax rate of up to 37 percent (p. 221). In 2020 an *FT* Leader explained that carry was also taxed as capital gain in the UK, the rate then being 28% rather than the 45% top rate of income tax. 'The result has been to foster a generation of buyout billionaires who have paid lower tax rates than their cleaners.' (FT Leader 2020b)

The relatively high power of the incentives for the PE managers can be compared with the rewards for a leading practitioner of the old conglomerate acquisition model. Mr Welch,[2] CEO of GE for twenty-one years, is estimated to have received between $450 mn and $800 mn over his whole employment by GE (Gryta and Mann 2020, pp. 319–20). He was head of the biggest company in the world, and 'Manager of the Century'. But his compensation does not come close to that of the 23 PE billionaires reported by Phalippou (2020), not counting the prospective billionaires whose gains have not yet all crystallised: 'the estimated total performance fee [carry] collected by these funds is estimated to be $230 bn, most of which goes to a relatively small number of individuals', notes Phalippou.

Phalippou (2020) provides a revealing analysis of the distribution of gains from one fund created by Blackstone, a leading US private equity business:

> An investment made by a 2006 vintage fund generated $2.6bn of carry for the PE firm (plus at least $685mn of management fees), $150mn for the CEO ($100mn for rest of senior management), $5bn for selling shareholders and $470mn of direct acquisition costs (plus other professional service fees).

Does this mean that PE's new model—combining tighter supervision of the managers of acquired businesses with the fruits of financial

---

1   Sometimes a percentage of profits above a threshold.
2   The 'Neutron Jack' of Chapter 1.

engineering (distorted by limited liability, tax breaks and a rigged debt market), and with the enhanced incentives (and privileged tax) for executives—overturns the statistical finding that makes the rapid growth in merger activity since the 1970s so mysterious—the failure of most mergers to enhance performance? Phalippou's analysis of the performance of the PE industry more generally suggests not. He concludes that 'Private Equity funds have returned about the same as public equity indices since *at least* 2006.' The structure of PE deals and resultant gains to various stakeholders clearly create an incentive to engage in M&A activity. But it is not clear whether the PE model has typically produced operating gains. PE firms have responded to Phalippou's findings with indignation, claiming that other performance measures show them in a more favourable light. But Phalippou has provided a compelling critique of alternative measures such as the internal rate of return, noting that '[i]n a complex environment riddled with multiple layers of agency conflicts, misleading information can and does proliferate.' The next chapters explore information problems in the wider M&A market which help perpetuate mergers that yield no gain in operating performance.

Section C

Information Asymmetry

Incomplete information or misinformation afflict the M&A process in a number of ways. The limited information available to stock investors can give rise to volatility in share prices, more than is warranted by the variation shown in the subsequent earnings they are supposed to represent. Acquirers may take advantage of unwarranted increases in the price of their own shares, which enable them to buy a target with those inflated shares—a bargain. Or again, if management know that the stock market, based on its limited information, is undervaluing a potential target they have the opportunity to make a capital gain by acquisition. In neither case has the motive anything to do with increasing operating profit (Chapter 8). Then, when outsiders do not enjoy access to the same information as the insiders, executives of would-be acquirers can engineer a higher share price by creative accounting: again, they can benefit from an acquisition which offers no operating gains (Chapter 9). The same outcome may be achieved by issuing biased earnings forecasts of the earnings the combination would achieve after merger—to inflate the price of shares offered in exchange for the target. Once the deal has been agreed, the accounting procedures for combining the accounts of the two firms have offered rich opportunities to flatter the earnings reported post-merger (Chapter 9). These procedures can help sustain a feedback loop, where inflated earnings facilitate a merger which offers further opportunities to flatter earnings, setting the scene for another deal... (Chapter 10). Finally, if the merger fails badly, accounting regulations sometimes leave sufficient flexibility for the CEO who led the merger to conceal the damage, or for his successor to exaggerate it (Chapter 9).

8. Inefficient Mergers in an 'Efficient' Market

acquisitions are made by overvalued acquirers of relatively less overvalued targets. (Shleifer and Vishny 2003, p. 305)

This chapter advances a claim which is contentious and at first sight counter-intuitive: that an 'efficient' stock market can facilitate and stimulate M&A which brings no gain in operating profit for the merging firms, and sometimes losses.[1]

Theory

Our students find it confusing that in one course they are being taught that the stock market is 'efficient'—indeed many academic studies rely on this proposition in interpreting movements in share prices—but in another course they are being told that the stock market sometimes enables or even induces inefficient mergers. An important reason for the confusion is that there are several different concepts of stock market 'efficiency' in economics; writers do not always make it clear which one they are using; and sometimes, one suspects, we find it too convenient to slide from one concept to another in order to make our arguments more compelling—claiming more generality than is warranted for our conclusions. To minimise confusion in this and the next chapter, we'll outline which concepts of efficiency we are considering at each point.[2]

---

[1] We are not claiming that stock markets such as the American and British are reliably efficient in any of the senses discussed below. Rather, the argument is that, *even if these markets were efficient in these senses, they would facilitate and stimulate some M&A which yielded no gain in operating profit. If the markets are inefficient, the arguments hold* a fortiori.

[2] These conceptual issues are further explored and explained particularly clearly by Dissanaike (2010).

© 2022 Geoff Meeks and J. Gay Meeks, CC BY-NC-ND 4.0 https://doi.org/10.11647/OBP.0309.08

Two Nobel Laureates are helpful. Nobel Laureate James Tobin (1984) spells out a hierarchy of concepts of 'efficiency':

1. The least ambitious is his 'information arbitrage efficiency'. Share prices in a market that is efficient in this sense take full account of the available information. On average an investor cannot gain by trading on the basis of available information. Within this category there is a crucial further distinction which we pursue in the next chapter. This was spelled out very clearly by Nobel Laureate Eugene Fama (1970):

   i.   a market which is informationally 'semi-strong' efficient incorporates all *publicly available* information, and

   ii. a 'strong form' informationally efficient market incorporates *all information, including inside* information.

In Chapter 9 we explore how, with semi-strong efficiency the selective or biased release of inside information distorts the M&A market, enabling deals which depress operating gains.

2. More ambitious is Tobin's next category, 'fundamental valuation efficiency'. In a market which achieves this level of efficiency the price of an asset (in our case a share in a business) 'accurately reflects the future payments to which the asset gives title'. In this chapter we consider how deviations from this ideal of efficiency (but conformity with semi-strong information efficiency) can lead to M&A which fails to yield extra operating profit, or even leads to reduced profit.

Estimates of the 'future payments to which the asset gives title' are challenging for shareholders. They are entitled just to a share of whatever earnings the business generates over the rest of its lifetime, about which there will typically be many 'known unknowns' and some 'unknown unknowns'.[3] The lack of hard information about the many future years that are relevant can make for swings of sentiment. And these can translate into substantial short-term swings in share price (Botsari and Meeks 2018). Such swings in share price attract speculators into the market. And Tobin quotes a famous piece by Keynes (1936) suggesting that in markets with negligible fundamentals (great uncertainty) speculative profits can be made from successfully guessing the sentiment of other

---

3   Terms familiar from and usually attributed to Donald Rumsfeld's famous response in a Defense Department meeting in 2002, but also used earlier by others in specialist risk assessments.

speculators. Keynes likened professional investment in the stock market to:

> [...] those newspaper competitions in which the competitors have to pick out the six prettiest faces from a hundred photographs, the prize being awarded to the competitor whose choice most nearly corresponds to the average preferences of the competitors as a whole; so that each competitor has to pick, not those faces which he himself finds prettiest, but those which he thinks likeliest to catch the fancy of the other competitors, all of whom are looking at the problem from the same point of view [...] [We] have reached the third degree where we devote our intelligences to anticipating what average opinion expects the average opinion to be. (p. 156)

And, in Tobin's words, this speculation 'multiplies several-fold the underlying fundamental variability of dividends and earnings'. Tobin writes that the 'speculations on the speculations of other speculators who are doing the same thing [...] dominate, of course, the pricing of assets with negligible fundamentals'. Such assets can include shares in merging firms.

Evidence

Nobel Laureate Robert J. Shiller (2001, 2015) has assembled compelling evidence that the fluctuations in stock market prices are indeed much greater than is warranted by the variation in subsequent real dividends which they would reflect in a market which was fundamentally valuation efficient. And at the level of the individual firm, evidence has accumulated that 'investors have overly optimistic expectations about the cash flows of some firms and overly pessimistic expectations about the cash flows of other firms' (Engelberg et al. 2019). This follows earlier evidence of 'overreaction'—stock market prices reacting more positively than is warranted to good news and vice versa (Chopra et al. 1992, Dissanaike 1997).

Work by Scherer (1988) links such findings to the M&A market. He cites numbers provided by Black (1986, p. 533) in his Presidential Address to the American Finance Association, when he imputes to the market a rather modest standard for valuation efficiency:

> [We] might define an efficient market as one in which price is within a
> factor of 2 of value, i.e., the price is more than half of value and less than
> twice value. The factor of 2 is arbitrary, of course. Intuitively, though, it
> seems reasonable to me, in the light of sources of uncertainty about value
> and the strength of the forces tending to cause price to return to value.
> By this definition, I think almost all markets are efficient almost all of the
> time. 'Almost all' means at least 90 per cent.

Take one extreme case where, in Black's account, the share price of a
business in an efficient market is temporarily almost 'twice value',
and the executives of the business—possessing more complete inside
information—are confident of this overvaluation. Then the business has
the opportunity to use its own inflated shares as currency for buying
other businesses whose share price just reflects 'value'. This can be in
the interests of the acquirer's shareholders even if the deal offers zero
or negative operating gains: they make a gain on the deal at the expense
of the target's shareholders who don't have the information to recognise
that the acquirer's shares they receive in payment are overvalued.

Of course, overvaluation is often a market-wide phenomenon—the
'hot' stock markets, the 'boom' and 'hysteria' phases of bubbles famously
described by Minsky (1986). The swings in sentiment in markets with
asymmetric information are familiar from other branches of economics.
In his analysis of the 2008 financial crash Wolf (2015, p. 122) revives
Galbraith's (1997) lively account of the cyclical changes in deceit and
distrust in capital markets:

> In good times people are relaxed, trusting, and money is plentiful. But
> even though money is plentiful, there are always many people who
> need more. Under these circumstances the rate of embezzlement grows,
> the rate of discovery falls off, and the bezzle [deceit] increases rapidly.
> In depressions all this is reversed. Money is watched with a narrow,
> suspicious eye. The man who handles it is assumed to be dishonest until
> he proves himself otherwise.

This cyclical pattern helps to explain a surprising feature of M&A—firms
make more acquisitions when the price of the targets is unusually high
(Botsari and Meeks 2018). If you are looking to buy assets, you would
normally benefit from buying them when their price is depressed. But
Shleifer and Vishny (2003) explain the economic logic of buying in hot
markets as quoted at the head of the chapter: 'acquisitions are made

by overvalued acquirers of relatively less overvalued targets' (p. 305). It can still be rational to embark on share for share acquisitions which offer zero or negative operating gains, provided that the acquirers' shares are more overvalued than the target's. Andrade et al. (2001) report that almost 60% of M&A in the 1990s was financed entirely by share exchange (before the more recent domination of debt financing). Statistical evidence supporting the proposition of Shleifer and Vishny is provided by, for example, Dong et al. (2006) and Gregory and Bi (2011).

Then take the opposite extreme case in Black's account—a depressed market where a company's share price has been driven down to a little more than 'half of value'. This represents an opportunity for a potential bidder, even if that bidder's own share price is equally depressed. In this case, the deal should be financed with cash (cheap and easy to borrow in recent years, as we discussed in earlier chapters).

So in the financial crisis of 2007–2009, Bob Diamond was able at the height of the panic to buy for Barclays a large component of insolvent Lehman, yielding a 'day one accounting gain' of several billion dollars (Thayer 2010). Violent movements in another financial market targeted by speculators—for foreign exchange—create opportunities for M&A. In the immediate aftermath of the unexpected 2016 UK referendum vote for Brexit, Japanese SoftBank's Masayoshi Son 'bet with a big size', acquiring the British semiconductor and software design company, Arm Holdings. One month after the Brexit vote the further fall in sterling had meant that such British assets cost Japanese buyers almost 30% less than they did a year earlier (Vincent 2016a). And more recently, in the 2020 pandemic, England and Kerr (2020) reported that 'Gulf sovereign wealth funds including Saudi Arabia's Public Investment Fund [PIF] and Abu Dhabi's Mubadala are mobilizing to buy assets whose valuations have been hardest hit by the outbreak.' Again, Thomas and Hollinger (2021) quote a fund manager in the wake of the pandemic and Brexit: 'There are a swath of well-managed UK mid-caps that trade at well below replacement cost'; and note that 'this has made them vulnerable to opportunistic bids'. In each case, the buyers stood to make a large capital gain. There need not have been any operating gain to be had from the deal—indeed the capital gain might have been sufficient to outweigh a significant operating loss. The transaction could have been zero-sum or negative-sum.

Such deals may just be taking advantage of the market's swings between excessive pessimism and excessive optimism. But given the fragility of valuations by the imperfectly-informed market, Shleifer and Vishny argue that bidders can exploit their superior, insider access to (and control of) information in order to inflate the value of their equity and make bargain acquisitions. We explore this process in the next chapter.

9. The Accountant's M&A Cookbook[1]

[M&A is]: The Black Hole in British accounting
　(David Tweedie, Chair of UK Accounting Standards Board, quoted in Smith 1996)

a powerful incentive for firms to get their equity overvalued, so that they can make acquisitions with stock (Shleifer and Vishny, p. 309).

Suppose you were an executive or adviser constructing a team to deliver a merger which offered no operating gains and would incur significant transaction costs: it was motivated by the benefits for the executive and/or adviser that we discussed in Chapters 2 to 7. Then you would have been well-advised to include in your team a clever 'creative' accountant. They are expensive—in the UK a partner of a Big4 accounting firm is typically paid towards a million pounds a year (O'Dwyer 2021). But they have been able (legally) to do much to smooth the CEO's path to a merger which brought no operating gains.

To secure support and finance for the deal on favourable terms the creative accountant should be able to manage the accounts so as to flatter earnings ahead of the offer—raising expectations of the dividends after the merger and the share price ahead of the bid. To the same end, she will also ensure that optimistic forecasts are issued of the earnings which are expected if the acquisition goes ahead. If the deal does go ahead, then, under current rules, the creative accountant will be able to record the integration of the target in ways which will inflate post-merger earnings reported in the published accounts. This is particularly helpful to acquirer CEOs pursuing acquisitions which deliver operating losses (see Chapter 2): the creative accountant can

---

1　This chapter draws on Meeks and Meeks (2013).

© 2022 Geoff Meeks and J. Gay Meeks, CC BY-NC-ND 4.0　　https://doi.org/10.11647/OBP.0309.09

mask poor underlying returns in such a failing merger. In the next chapter we explore a potential feedback loop, or 'virtuous' circle, for serial acquirers, combining the creative accounting pre-merger with that for integration: spurious profits ahead of a bid secure a share for share acquisition on favourable terms, and the acquisition enables the accountant to create spurious profits after merger, setting the scene for the next deal.

Should the merger fail to deliver the earnings gains promised when the purchase consideration was decided, the creative accountant may be able to avoid or delay an impairment charge reducing profits in the income statement, which would embarrass the acquirer's CEO. Alternatively, she may be able to exaggerate such a charge if a new CEO (the accountant's new boss) wants to discredit her predecessor and flatter her own reputation. Finally in this chapter, we show how—if your business needs more intangible assets—anomalies in the current accounting rules mean that your reported earnings over time can be substantially higher if you buy the intangibles as part of an acquisition rather than generate them internally. As an aside in Appendix 2 we also report on a highly sophisticated past M&A accounting device used to hide a business failure—in our illustration, losses on speculative investments. But beware: unlike the other devices we explore, this one was fraudulent, so it doesn't make it into the chapter. Unless you can muzzle whistleblowers, you may end up in court (as the perpetrators did, albeit very many years later).

In the rest of this chapter and in Appendix 2 we give many examples of creative accounting around M&A. Because most people have limited interest in the intricacies of accounting, we have put much of the detail in the appendix and given just the gist in the chapter. The examples are drawn from different countries and different periods, but especially the UK and US in the last four decades. Standard-setters have in some cases been able subsequently to eliminate particular devices we describe. We advise any readers tempted to try one of the devices to take advice on whether they are still permissible.

Creative Accounting ahead of the Offer

In reporting manipulation of the accounts we note Griffiths' (1986) guidance many years ago: 'the hallmark of [effective] creative accounting is that it does not involve fraud'. It should be discreetly and judiciously employed; it should not get you into jail; it should enhance rather than damage your reputation. The opportunities for such legal and effective earnings management arise particularly in areas where insider executives, in daily contact with their employees, their markets and their trading partners, enjoy an information advantage over outsiders, even including auditors, and where the insiders have to make accounting estimates requiring judgement. Then, if or when the estimates are not confirmed by subsequent outcomes, it may not be possible to discriminate between the role of unanticipated external developments outside the executives' control, on the one hand, and intentional bias in the executives' estimates, on the other. In these circumstances, the 'creative' executives can escape censure. As Dechow et al. (2011) argue, 'the more assets on the balance sheet that are subject to changes in assumptions and forecasts, the greater the manager's flexibility to manage short-term earnings' (p. 19).

If outsiders cannot identify or quantify the resulting earnings management then in a semi-strong efficient market for capital (one which can only be relied upon to reflect public information—Chapter 8), skilful upward manipulation of earnings can raise the share price. If the acquiring management then offer their own (inflated) shares in exchange for those of the target, they can secure the deal on unduly favourable terms. The target shareholders might not have agreed to the deal had the acquirers' share prices not been manipulated. The acquirers' shareholders gain from the sleight of hand—perhaps enough to compensate for the transaction costs of the deal and some operating losses afterwards. The acquirers' executives mostly gain from the deal (Chapter 2), and their advisers almost always do (Chapter 3).

Historically, creative accounting has been just one of the weapons bidders have employed to hoodwink investors. Kynaston lists further 'methods of deception' employed by acquiring businesses in the late-twentieth century to support artificially the price of their own company's stock. In relation to the strategies of one aggressive bidder,

Robert Maxwell, the methods included 'changes of year-ends, backdated agreements, imaginary goodwill, trading between public and private companies, inflated stock valuations, returnable 'sales', bogus profit forecasts, furtive disposals of shares, ...' (p. 383). Lawmakers and regulators have worked to curb these abuses: in the UK, many egregious creative accounting devices were outlawed in the 1990s by the pioneering Accounting Standards Board. The US and international standards boards (FASB and IASB) have also worked continually to contain creative accounting. But some devices arise from unavoidable characteristics of accounting; some have been retained against the wishes of the standard-setters, following lobbying by business; and innovative new accounting devices have been developed when old ones have been outlawed.

Past and current creative accounting devices have often been able to mislead investors in a semi-strong efficient market. Often they involve taking an unduly optimistic view of future outcomes when executives review the allocation of costs or revenues to different accounting years. Or they focus on the valuation of assets or liabilities in the balance sheet at the end of the accounting period, where this affects the profits recognised for that period.

A supplier of capital goods or a construction firm partway through a major multi-year contract for which total payment was fixed might take an over-optimistic view of the further costs which would be incurred to finish the project, thereby inflating the profits reported in the short term. Where such manipulation is not available, a business might engage in 'channel stuffing'—persuading a customer to take a shipment earlier than they would normally choose, ahead of the supplier's accounting year-end—swelling sales, receivables and profits in that accounting-year. (When we asked a group of managers in our executive education course how many had been asked by their employers to engineer such an acceleration of revenue as the year-end approached, the majority raised their hands.)

A tech business which holds inventory liable to obsolescence has each year to review its value, and write it down if it can't be sold for what it has cost to produce. This requires managers' judgement. Understate the write down and this year's profit is inflated. Overstate the write-down and then succeed in selling it another year for more than its written-down value, and profits are moved to another year. Businesses which sell goods or services on credit (or banks which lend) need to take a view at the year-end of how many debtors will actually pay: a more optimistic judgement will result in higher profits for the accounting year. Then, last century in the UK, until the ASB intervened, a company could raise funds via complex financial instruments in which interest payments were end-loaded, boosting reported earnings in the early years (Tweedie, Cook and Whittington forthcoming).

The common feature in most of these measures is that the executives are better equipped than their auditors, let alone their shareholders, to make these estimates, and that they are generally not transparent to outsiders. Even where auditors are uncomfortable with a device being used by an auditee, they face a dilemma over whether to challenge its use unless they have a clear mandate from company law or the regulators. The former chairman of the UK Accounting Standards Board and the International Accounting Standards Board explains: '...if you look at the individual partners, the senior partners probably had two big clients each. Well, you lose one of those and your value to the firm is questioned. So there's huge pressure not to lose a client.' (Tweedie, Cook and Whittington)

Illustrations of such accounting devices are provided in Appendix 2—for Xerox, GE, Carillion, Coca Cola, Cisco, Tesco and others.

But there's something puzzling in all this. If, to succeed in misleading investors and boosting share prices in a semi-strong efficient market, creative accounting has to be opaque—outsiders can't see through it—how do we outsiders know that it is happening?

One source we draw on in Appendix 2 is the whistleblower, an insider who reveals the sleights of hand—as in the case of Tesco's understatement of payables, or Olympus's cover-up of losses on investments. A second source recalls one of Warren Buffett's many famous investor quotes: 'It's only when the tide goes out that you discover who's been swimming naked'. When firms go bust, the administrators or liquidators suddenly have access to the internal records and to the employees of such firms. These often reveal accounting manipulation—as in the cases of Carillion, Coloroll, Enron and WorldCom discussed elsewhere in this book—and sometimes insiders spill the beans where there are official public enquiries into a failure which has caused widespread damage (Chapter 11 gives an example). The third source is statistical analysis of large numbers of accounts. In Schipper's (1989) words as to why researchers are able to observe earnings management while users of the manipulated accounts can't: 'a researcher using large historical data sets might be able to document statistically a pattern of behavior consistent with earnings management within the sample, without being able to say with confidence whether earnings were managed for any particular firm in the sample' (p. 97).

In relation to statistical analysis of large historical datasets, much of the research has focused on creative accounting ahead of major financial events, such as IPOs or seasoned equity offerings, or—our concern—share for share acquisitions. We earlier quoted Shleifer and Vishny (2003) on the 'powerful incentive for firms to get their equity overvalued, so that they can make acquisitions with stock' on favourable terms. The emphasis on major financial events is because in the ordinary run of business the benefit from using most of the creative accounting devices we report is likely to be short-lived: many of these devices just bring forward into this year's accounts profits from a future year: any gain this year will be at the expense of profits in one or more future years. And on top of that, if the manipulation becomes known, the executive's credibility will thereafter be dented. But creative accounting ahead of a major financial event such as merger offers the opportunity to lock in a gain—by securing a transaction on terms made more favourable by the temporary inflation of earnings. Moreover, in the case of M&A, we show in Appendix 2 that a clever accountant has sometimes created reported earnings 'out of thin air' in the course of an acquisition, to conceal the negative repercussions of the earlier inflation of short-term profit. This makes it less likely that the executives are 'found out'.

Statistical research on acquirers' use of earnings management ahead of, and to facilitate, M&A has been completed for several countries and periods in recent decades (Erikson and Wang 1999; Louis 2004; Botsari and Meeks 2008, 2018; Gong et al. 2008; Higgins 2013; Botsari 2020). Researchers have found evidence of earnings management (on average) ahead of share for share deals; and evidence that this succeeded in artificially boosting the share price of the acquirer ahead of the deal. By contrast, in cash deals earnings management ahead of the offer is not typically observed (the target's shareholders do not in this case have to be persuaded to accept the acquirer's shares in return for their own).

The pre-bid earnings management is associated particularly with 'hot' stock markets, when M&A markets are most active (Chapter 8).

Great Expectations: Forecasts of Post-merger Earnings

A statistical approach is also valuable in identifying and assessing a second means of flattering accounting information in order to secure advantageous terms for stock-for-stock acquisitions: issuing forecasts of earnings gains from the combination. There are currently few regulatory requirements to issue such earnings forecasts: in our samples of large US deals, forecasts were not published by all bidders.[2] And only a minority issued the most challenging 'point forecasts', committing to a particular earnings increase; the remainder issued qualitative forecasts—e.g. 'the deal will be accretive to earnings'.

On average the subsequent outcomes were markedly lower than the earnings per share (EPS) forecast provided by managers, where available: in the majority of cases the executives got it systematically wrong and over-estimated future earnings following the merger (Amel-Zadeh and Meeks 2020b). This finding would come as no surprise to legendary investor Warren Buffett, whose 1982 letter to shareholders of his Berkshire Hathaway commented: 'While deals often fail in practice, they never fail in projections.' And it is consistent with recent research by the Federal Reserve Bank of New York (Acharya et al. 2022), which concludes that 'M&A announcements are usually accompanied by rosy forecasts about synergies and growth, and, more importantly, a promise to reduce the debt taken on to finance the acquisition. Data indicate that most of these projections were, ex post, not realised'.

Was the stock market impressed by these over-optimistic forecasts? Another analysis (Amel-Zadeh and Meeks 2019) found that in stock-for-stock acquisitions, bidders which had a record of issuing reliable routine earnings—and then issued an optimistic forecast of earnings expected after an acquisition—secured a higher probability of completing the deal, faster completion, and a lower acquisition premium. So it is advisable for the creative accountant to build confidence ahead—by ensuring that earnings are managed such that routine forecasts prove accurate in the years immediately preceding a bid.

---

2   In the UK some forward-looking financial information has to be provided in some cases to shareholders under Takeover Panel and Listing Rules.

Before the deal is completed the highly skilled creative accountant will have prepared a plan aiming to flatter earnings that are reported afterwards. She will not find this difficult. Accounting rules for assimilating targets in the acquirers' accounts have offered rich opportunities to flatter subsequent earnings. We discuss these in the next section.

We leave unanswered an interesting question about forecasts: does the evidence on unfulfilled forecasts reflect deception or just self-delusion on the part of the bidder executives?

Accounting for the Deal: Creating Spurious Post-merger Earnings

The key accounting device currently available at the time of merger to manipulate post-merger earnings was neatly expressed some time ago by the senior technical partner of one of the major audit firms: 'the trick is to attribute the lowest possible values to the net assets acquired, and correspondingly the highest possible value to the residual goodwill [...] the smaller the assets which remain to be charged against profits the better the post-acquisition results will appear' (Paterson 1988, p. 43).[3]

If, for example, inventory is marked down excessively, reported profit will be inflated when that inventory is subsequently sold. If machinery is marked down, depreciation charges will be lower in subsequent years—again, profits are inflated. Absent goodwill impairment, the higher allocation to goodwill when other assets are marked down will not lead to any subsequent charge against profits: amortisation of purchased goodwill in the profit and loss account (reducing profits year by year) is now generally disallowed for listed companies.[4] This means that marking down the fair value of the assets on acquisition, allocating more of the purchase consideration to the (residual) goodwill account, can, in effect, create a 'cookie jar' from which the accountant can draw

---

3   This argument applies in those regimes where goodwill is not amortised, and where impairment is not subsequently triggered. In some jurisdictions, amortisation is allowed for private companies. By 2020 FASB were minded to reintroduce the amortisation of goodwill (Lugo 2020).

4   The qualification to this is that goodwill may under current FASB/IASB arrangements be impaired.

extra profits in years following the acquisition. Illustrations are provided in Appendix 2.

The sums involved can be enormous. For example, when Vodafone paid £101 billion for Mannesmann, purchased goodwill represented £83 billion of the total.

There is a paradox with such devices. At first sight, these downward adjustments of the value of the target's net assets when it is recorded in the acquirer's books appear consistent with the conservative/prudent/cautious approach traditionally drilled into accountants from the beginning of their training. As the past Chairman of the ASB and IASB, and scourge of creative accountants, Sir David Tweedie commented, 'you can't stop people writing things down' (Tweedie and Whittington 2020, p. 70). But the accounting model means that the consequence for future years can be anything but conservative/prudent/cautious: subsequent earnings are over-stated.

Artificially enhancing earnings at this point in the M&A process can serve at least three purposes for the acquirer's CEO. First it can hide the hit to reported profits that would follow those creative accounting devices which—ahead of the merger—had 'borrowed' earnings from a future period. Second, it can boost the acquiring executives' own compensation where that is contractually tied to profit measures such as earnings per share—discussed in Chapter 2. And third, it can set the scene for another acquisition on terms unduly favourable to the acquirer. This is important to the next chapter's discussion of virtuous (vicious?) circles in serial acquisition programmes. They represent perhaps the most sophisticated expression of the creative accountant's art.

Creative Accounting Post-merger

Creative accounting activities during merger may then leave the acquirer with a swollen figure for purchased goodwill in its balance sheet. This 'asset' represents the anticipation, or hope, or pretence, of above average returns during future years. If that anticipation is disappointed, listed companies following current IASB or FASB standards are supposed to reduce the goodwill total with an 'impairment' charge to the P&L.

At first sight, impairment seems superior to amortisation as a method of recording the depletion of purchased goodwill. In theory, it represents the <u>actual</u> diminution of the expected earnings underpinning goodwill. And that would seem preferable to amortisation's mechanical, formulaic allocation to each year's P&L of past expenditure on goodwill. But there are strong motives and ample means to manipulate goodwill impairment.

On motives, Hans Hoogervorst, Chairman of IASB, has argued:

> in practice, entities may be hesitant to impair goodwill, so as to avoid giving the impression that they made a bad investment decision. Newly appointed CEOs, on the other hand, have a strong incentive to recognize hefty impairments on their predecessor's acquisitions. (KPMG 2014, p. 5)

Chapter 1 and Appendix 1 give evidence on the prevalence of mergers that were 'bad investment decisions'. Then Appendix 2 gives examples— for Vodafone and HP—of 'hefty impairments on their predecessor's acquisitions'. Such impairments avoid future impairments which would depress earnings on the new executive's watch; and, by depressing earnings at the point of succession, they secure a lower base point against which the newcomer's earnings will be judged.

On means, manipulating goodwill impairment is one of the easiest tasks facing the creative accountant. Appendix 2 gives more detail. Impairment requires a forecast of earnings long into the future; but we earlier reported the inaccuracy of even short-term forecasts. And executives enjoy considerable discretion over the models used to prepare forecasts—inevitable because of the great variation across companies in business models. Then how do you apportion future earnings between the acquirer and the target when the rationale of many deals is to integrate the two? And how do you apportion future earnings between the intangible goodwill purchased with the target and the intangible goodwill already generated internally by the acquirer and that subsequently generated by the merged firm? That distinction, between acquired and internally generated intangibles, is not just important to the impairment calculation: it is part of a much wider challenge for accounting—and opportunity for creative accountants—discussed in the next section.

The Intangibles Anomaly

Intangible assets are one of the most treasured ingredients in the accountant's M&A cookbook. Take a very simple example where a business wants to possess intangibles such as customer loyalty or intellectual property worth $100 million. Suppose it could build up these assets by spending $10 million a year on marketing or R&D for ten years (depressing profits by $10 m p.a.). Or it could buy these assets in the course of an acquisition for a single payment of $100 m. Unlike the $10 m a year spent on internal generation, that $100 m payment would not under current accounting rules be charged against profit as an expense, but would be recorded as the acquisition of an asset. If the asset did not qualify as 'separable' it would typically be recorded as purchased goodwill. And, under present accounting conventions, provided it was not subsequently 'impaired' (written down because it was deemed to have diminished in value), it would never be charged to the profit and loss account, diminishing profit. Meeks and Meeks (2020a) explain and illustrate the process in more detail.

This example shares with the earlier ones the characteristic that accounting conventions cause the same economic activities to be reported for participants in M&A in ways which produce very different values for reported earnings from those prevailing in the absence of M&A. The underlying issue was described by the American Accounting Association (AAA) in 1991: 'The inclusion of purchased goodwill and the omission of internally-generated goodwill is one of accounting's greatest anomalies'. The anomaly identified by the AAA continues, though on a bigger scale than in 1991 because purchased goodwill has been growing exceptionally quickly since then with the surge in M&A; and spending on intangibles representing internally generated goodwill has also expanded at unprecedentedly high rates (see Appendix 2).

There is an irony in all this. In Appendix 2 we report the complaint by an executive lobbying Congress that, if amortisation of goodwill were required, it would 'stifle technology development, impede capital formation and slow job creation'. But actually, under the regime secured by the business lobbyists, why would the CEO of a tech firm with funds to create intangibles spend years depressing reported earnings by generating the intangibles internally when she could just buy them 'ready-made' in an acquisition, with no hit to reported profit?

10. Feedback Loops

> Growth through continued acquisition is like a drug. The more successful each deal is, the bigger the next deal has to be to make an impact and continue the pattern of growth. The take-over vehicles not only found that bigger and bigger take-overs were necessary to maintain profits growth, but also found a series of techniques associated with acquisitions and disposals which could be used to boost profits. (Smith 1996, p. 19)

An extraordinarily frank account of such a circular and cumulative feedback model of serial acquisition was provided in Lynch (1971) by a CEO who deployed it many decades ago. He quotes the CEO of Contek (not its real name):

> Obviously, the one reason that we can justify this kind of an investment is the high price-earnings ratio placed on Contek by the market, which reflects continued confidence in our growth program […] Because of our high multiple and because of the relative size of our respective operations, this projected earnings [of the target] will strongly enhance our market value. This in turn will make it possible for us to raise additional capital to acquire other companies and generally to fulfil the growth which is expected of us.
>
> An interesting consequence of the transaction is the fact that this projected earnings [of the target] added to current earnings alone would raise total earnings per share from $0.61 to $1.0. At our current [price-earnings] multiple, the effect would be to raise our stock price to $30 per share from its current value of $18.

Contek made fifteen acquisitions in a six-year period studied by Lynch. Sales rose thirty-six-fold. 93% of the sales at the end of the period came from the newly acquired subsidiaries. Searching for operating gains, Lynch analysed the accounting profits (net, before tax) on the book value of total capital for Contek subsidiaries: he found either 'no improvement or declines on either a simple or weighted average basis'.

© 2022 Geoff Meeks and J. Gay Meeks, CC BY-NC-ND 4.0 https://doi.org/10.11647/OBP.0309.10

And yet earnings per share—the performance measure still prominent in companies' annual reports, press and analyst commentaries, and executive bonus contracts—increased from 15 cents to $2.30.

Gryta and Mann (2020) in their study of the rise and decline of the US giant GE drew attention to a similar potential 'virtuous' circle in merger activity. They note that the 'all important' (p. 48) performance metric followed by Wall Street was earnings per share (EPS—in Chapter 2 we noted its role in performance-related pay contracts for senior executives). And they go on to explore the powerful role of M&A in boosting earnings per share, whether or not the acquisitions succeeded in securing operating gains:

> A steady stream of acquisitions fed the earnings momentum. GE could use its unusually high price-to-earnings ratio [PE] for an industrial company as high value currency to pay for deals. By acquiring companies with a lower price-to-earnings ratio, GE was getting an automatic earnings boost.
>
> As an example, if GE was trading at a price-to-earnings ratio of 40, that meant that, if its stock was $40, it was earning $1 per share every year. If GE then bought a company with a price-to-earnings ratio of 10— that company was earning $4... for every $40 of stock...

In relation to our question of why firms can get away with mergers that fail, Gryta and Mann's arithmetic means then that there could be a gain in earnings per share even if the deal led to a decline in the target's operating profits.

Gryta and Mann go on:

> GE shares weren't going to stay valued that way forever. It would have to do more deals or use other methods to produce earnings. One way to do this was by contorting accounting rules to make acquisitions seem even more profitable. (p. 50)

GE certainly 'did more deals': almost 1,000 acquisitions in the two-decade tenure of CEO Welch (Gryta and Mann), some 700 in the sixteen-year tenure of his successor Immelt. And Gryta and Mann recount the creative accounting devices they deployed to manage earnings (all familiar from Chapter 9's cookbook): tweaking the expected future costs of multi-period contracts (p. 7); fudging the value of inventory (p. 29); channel stuffing (p. 31, p. 91); writing down the 'fair value' of acquired assets (p. 50).

Many of the 1700 businesses bought by Messrs Welch and Immelt were subsequently sold off. By 2018, GE's market value was a small fraction of its level at the millennium, and—having been the longest surviving member—GE was removed from the Dow Jones Industrial Average (Dissanaike et al. 2022). And in 2021, CEO Larry Culp announced that what remained of the company was to be broken up (Edgecliffe-Johnson et al. 2021)

An extreme example of the feedback model of serial acquisition combined with creative accounting is provided by the British company Coloroll, analysed by Smith (1996). In the five years from its listing on the stock market in 1985 with a market value of £37 million Coloroll acquired fifteen companies at a cost of £400 million, one of those acquirees having itself made twenty-five acquisitions in the preceding four years.

Coloroll made aggressive use of the devices we outlined in the previous chapter. In particular it used acquisitions to create a cookie jar: the inventories and receivables of targets were written down, and restructuring provisions were created, artificially boosting reported profits following the acquisitions, creating favourable conditions for financing and securing further deals. In its final year, £52 million of 'profit' were drawn from the cookie jar—expenses were debited to the provisions account rather than to the profit and loss account, effectively swelling reported profit by that amount. Total reported profit for the year was £56 million. Had it not been for the provisions the management used, reported profit would have been just £4 million. Such examples prompted strong action by the Accounting Standards Board to curtail such use of restructuring provisions (Tweedie, Cook and Whittington forthcoming).

Apparently highly profitable according to the recent accounts, but heavily indebted, illiquid and in reality insolvent, Coloroll failed a few months later.

However, the ingenious architect of Coloroll's rise, Managing Director Philip Green, was not permanently lost to UK business. He plays an important role in the next chapter.

PART THREE

RESOLUTION: REVIEW AND REFORM

11. Exemplars of Failure

> Carillion's rise and spectacular fall was a story of recklessness, hubris and greed. Its business model was a relentless dash for cash, driven by acquisitions, rising debt, expansion into new markets and exploitation of suppliers. It presented accounts that misrepresented the reality of the business, and increased its dividend every year, come what may. Long term obligations, such as adequately funding its pension schemes, were treated with contempt. Even as the company very publicly began to unravel, the board was concerned with increasing and protecting generous executive bonuses. Carillion was unsustainable. The mystery is not that it collapsed, but that it lasted so long. (HoC 2018)

Before we turn to possible measures to reduce the extent of failure in the M&A market, it may be helpful to bring together most of the strands of the argument so far. Two cases already mentioned, one from the UK, one from the US, epitomise the activities which we have argued are associated with mergers that fail.

Carillion

In the UK case, the UK Parliamentary investigation produced a lucid account of this strategy and its consequences, from which the quote above is taken and from which most of our account is drawn (HoC 2018). Paragraphs from that report are referenced as HoC1, HoC2, and so on.

The story combines major acquisitions, financial failure, monopolistic/monopsonistic pressure on customers and suppliers, misinformation, moral hazard, huge costs to parties other than its executives and advisers, and influence at the very top of government. When it failed in 2018, Carillion was the second largest construction

© 2022 Geoff Meeks and J. Gay Meeks, CC BY-NC-ND 4.0 https://doi.org/10.11647/OBP.0309.11

company in the UK, with extensive activities overseas. It had built its position with M&A, heavy reliance on debt, and large, risky contracts.

One of the strands of our critique—in Chapter 1—was the disappointing outcome of much M&A. No better example could be offered than Carillion's diversifying acquisition of EAGA. Acquired in 2011 for £298 million, this subsidiary had by 2016, the year of its parent Carillion's death, generated cumulative losses of £260 million (HoC6).

Carillion offers a reminder also of Adam Smith's characterisation, in Chapter 1, of businessmen as engaged 'in a conspiracy against the public, or in some contrivance to raise prices'. Carillion grew not just by diversified M&A [EAGA], but also by the acquisition of major rivals in the same industry, to eliminate competitors and secure higher prices in large contracts—including Mowlem in 2006 for £350 m, and Alfred McAlpine in 2008 for £565 m.

This concentration of the industry exposed a major customer to the risks created by management. The UK government was such a customer of Carillion. When the contractor failed, work stopped on some 450 construction and service contracts with government. The public bore considerable costs as a result of Carillion's risk-taking, while shareholders' losses were capped by limited liability (Chapter 5). As one example of moral hazard, immediately the company failed, the government had to commit an extra £150 million just to maintain continuity in delivery of some services, and major projects such as hospital building stalled.

Carillion's risk exposure was exacerbated by its heavy use of borrowing—a preoccupation of Chapter 5. Borrowing rose from £242 m in 2009 to £689 m in 2016, when the debt-equity ratio reached 5.3 (HoC78). But ordinary borrowing was augmented by two sources of 'borrowing' which were on terms even more favourable than those already available to business generally because of the subsidies to borrowing provided by the tax system and the artificially low interest rates resulting from asymmetric monetary policy (Chapter 6). These sources were actually provided interest-free: and costs arising from the downside risks fell heavily on two interest groups: Carillion's suppliers and the members of the company's pension funds.

Chapter 5 reported on Carillion's monopsonistic power, achieved partly though M&A, which allowed it to demand from its suppliers interest-free funding which, as it turned out, carried very high risk. Suppliers had to wait up to four months for payment. And consequently, when Carillion failed, it owed around £2 billion to 30,000 suppliers, who 'will get little back from the liquidation' (HoC), and some of whom were likely themselves to be bankrupted as a result.

Carillion enjoyed a second source of funding on highly favourable terms: the members of its employee pension funds. Chapter 5 illustrated with BHS the way that obligations to a target's pension funds can be taken on by the acquirer, effectively reducing the outlay required to complete the merger.

When Carillion went into liquidation in 2018 it was responsible for thirteen defined benefit pension schemes. Responsibility for these schemes had mostly been accumulated in the course of M&A. For example, when acquiring Mowlem in 2006, Carillion assumed responsibility for the target's pension scheme (which had £33 million fewer assets than pension obligations); in the case of the scheme acquired with Alfred McAlpine in 2008 the shortfall was £123 million. Had the acquirer not taken responsibility for these schemes, the seller would have had to pay to clear the pensions deficit, and would presumably have demanded a corresponding extra sum from the buyer. In effect then, as in the BHS case, assuming responsibility for a target's pension scheme reduced the immediate purchase consideration for the acquisition.

Had Carillion taken out an extra loan to recompense the target for insuring the pension liability, Carillion would have had an extra interest bill in subsequent years. Instead, it had an obligation to make good the deficit—eventually. However, the adviser to the Trustee appointed to represent the interests of the pension fund members reported that Carillion had 'historically prioritized other demands on capital ahead of [pension] deficit reduction in order to grow earnings and support the share price' (HoC30). And the Chair of the Board of Trustees commented that Carillion's finance director regarded funding pension schemes as a 'waste of money' (HoC31). The parliamentary report argued that the Pensions Regulator was 'feeble' in allowing Carillion to neglect the pension fund.

After Carillion's failure, the national Pension Protection Fund had to assume responsibility for the pension scheme. Members received pensions from the Fund, but at a lower rate than they had been promised.

And the pension cuts still left the Fund with a shortfall of some £800 million to be paid from its reserves and from levies on its members (other employers with defined benefit pension schemes).

The CEO and finance director of Carillion escaped such losses: they were not members of the company's defined benefit pension scheme. Instead, they received annual contributions to personal 'defined contribution' schemes. The contributions in respect of 2016 were £231,000 and £163,000 respectively (HoC34; Carillion AR 2016, p. 66).

How did Carillion's stakeholders fare?

In truth, dividends should have been discontinued well ahead of the collapse. The executives masked the dire state of the company: in reporting the company's finances they were found by the parliamentary committees to have deployed creative accounting such as Chapter 9 describes.

Goodwill arising from M&A (which totalled £1.6 billion in 2016: HoC122) should have been impaired when expected profits did not materialise (Ford 2018). The impairment would have reduced profits and distributable reserves. But the executives exploited the discretion we discussed in Chapter 9 to delay any impairment. This, in combination with under-reporting (by around a billion pounds: HoC79) of losses on contracts, inflated reported earnings: Carillion had exploited the creative accounting opportunity outlined in Chapter 9 of front-loading the profits from multi-period contracts, and, when the profits were not sustained in the later years of contracts, had (finally) to make a provision in 2017 for £729 million. This device had enabled it to report higher distributable reserves, without which the continued growth in dividends would not have been permissible. During the tenure of finance director Richard Adams (2007 to December 2016), dividends to shareholders rose by 199% while (wholly inadequate) recovery payments to the under-funded pension schemes increased by just 12% (HoC18). Board members owned shares in the business and were direct beneficiaries of this policy. So—moral hazard in action—shareholders' interests were defended when the crisis deepened, at the expense of trade creditors and pensioners.

Consistent with Chapter 3, advisers' interests were protected too. Three days before the company was declared insolvent, resulting in huge losses to most creditors, Carillion took urgent steps to avoid their advisers (accountants, lawyers, etc.) being out of pocket, paying them £6.4 m (HoC127). If they had not rushed to do this, the advisers would have had to join the long queue of creditors hoping that the liquidators might eventually be able to pay them some portion of their claim.

The CFO, Mr Adams, who had been responsible for the company's finances since 2007, and will have been able to see the writing on the wall, made a well-timed departure from the company in December 2016. As the crisis had deepened, pay for the CEO and Mr Adams had increased sharply: from £1.8 m in 2014 to £3.0 m in 2016 for the two together (HoC61). Then Mr Adams sold all his shares in Carillion between March and May 2017, at an average price of 212 pence. By mid-July, as information on the firm's finances reached the market, the share price had fallen to 57 pence. The parliamentary committee described these as the 'actions of a man who knew exactly where the company was heading once it was no longer propped up by his accounting tricks.' (HoC105)

The reputations of most of the senior executives and non-executive directors of Carillion fared less well than their bank accounts when their actions were reviewed by the parliamentary committee. But this case also suggests that reputational damage endures less long than we expect, and that the political influence which often comes with leadership of a large business (Meeks, Meeks and Meeks forthcoming) can be surprisingly resilient. Overseeing the culture of misinformation and misaligned incentives at Carillion as senior non-executive director from 2011 and chairman of its board from 2014 was Philip Green. This Philip Green is not the same as Sir Philip Green of the BHS pension furore we discussed in Chapter 5 (we have re-checked this ten times as the coincidence seems hard to believe). Mr Green had also been at the centre of one of our important cases in Chapters 9 and 10, Coloroll. Coloroll was the serial acquirer which used grossly misleading accounting in the course of takeover—especially the notorious reorganisation provision—to create illusory profits, boosting its share price, and facilitating the next acquisition on unduly favourable terms. It too collapsed, leaving large debts unpaid and the pension fund in deficit, soon after reporting large profits. Mr Green was Coloroll's Managing Director. Following that episode at Coloroll, the Pensions Ombudsman made a finding of breach of trust and maladministration against him in 1994 (HoC60).

These achievements had earned him influence at the very top of government. In 2011, the year he joined Carillion's board, Mr Green was appointed adviser to the Prime Minister, Mr Cameron, on corporate responsibility (HoC60), and he held that position until 2016, alongside his powerful role at the head of Carillion.

GE

Our second example, GE, has appeared at several points in earlier chapters. It has almost every component of the explanations we have offered for ill-fated M&A: huge expenditures on M&A, sustained over decades, leading to a collapse in share price; high-powered financial incentives for the CEO; lucrative fees paid to financial advisers; heavy reliance on debt leading to government bailout; tax avoidance, creative accounting, and feedback loops.

In the last two decades of the twentieth century Chief Executive Jack Welch averaged roughly four acquisitions a month, about a thousand in total. His successor, Jeff Immelt, continued the strategy, acquiring some 700 businesses in his seventeen-year tenure.[1] In the early years this programme was accompanied by rising reported profits, and the stock market valuation of the business reached $600 billion in 2000; but by 2018 this had fallen to $98 billion (Edgecliffe-Johnson et al. 2021).

Messrs Welch and Immelt were well rewarded for their work: between $450 million and $800 million for Mr Welch while working at GE, and $168 million for Mr Immelt in his last eleven years to 2017.[2] Perks were generous too: we noted in Chapter 2 that Mr Immelt took two executive jets on his business travels. And they enjoyed the security afforded by enviable market power. For example, because of their dominant position in aircraft leasing they were able to insist on a 'GE only' tying policy when negotiating leases; they secured 65% of the market for large aircraft engines; and made money in aviation while their airline customers were struggling (Dissanaike et al. 2022).

Chapter 3 reported the benefits received by the banks which advised on, and raised funding for, GE's acquisitions. Banks including Goldman

---

1   Gryta and Mann (2020). They also divested a smaller but significant number.
2   Estimates by the *Wall Street Journal*, reported in Gryta and Mann (2020, pp. 319–20).

Sachs, JP Morgan and Morgan Stanley received more than $6 billion in fees from GE in the years of its decline since 2000.

Much of GE's expansion was accompanied by borrowing, with the attendant risks discussed in Chapter 5. The finance arm, GECS, had borrowings of over $200 billion in 2000.[3] The associated risks became evident in the financial crisis of 2008: GE had to call on government support—$139 billion of loan guarantees. It also had to resort to emergency sales of shares, at large discounts to recent prices—diluting the equity of existing shareholders.

(Legal) tax avoidance, the subject of Chapter 6, was also part of GE's strategy. Its Annual Report for 2011 explains: 'Our consolidated income tax rate is lower than the US statutory rate primarily because of benefits from lower-rated global operations, including the use of global funding structures [...] non-US income is subject to local country tax rates that are significantly below the 35% US statutory rate' (GE 2012, p. 37).

Chapter 10 reported GE's use of the creative accounting devices elaborated in Chapter 9, which flatter reported earnings, and assist the smoothing of earnings, an effect which finds favour with the stock market. This supported the feedback loop described in Chapter 10. Inflated earnings bolster the share price. This improves the terms on which an acquisition can be made. Then the acquisition itself creates fresh opportunities further to flatter earnings. Edgecliffe-Johnson et al. (2021) quote the director of the Securities and Exchange Commission's enforcement division: 'GE bent the accounting rules beyond the breaking point'.

---

3   GE (2001). For the business as a whole, borrowings equated to 46% of total assets (Dissanaike et al. 2022).

12. Remedies?

In this final chapter we recap the main lines of enquiry in our investigation of the mystery. We have identified a series of efficiency failings in the M&A market that help to explain merger activity that so often brings no operating gains. For each of the main failings we now suggest possible policy responses. The sequencing of the failings is different from that in the preceding chapters. There they were ordered according to underlying economic concepts—misaligned incentives, distorted financing, and asymmetric information. Here they are ordered according chiefly to which authorities would need to initiate the suggested changes, starting with government, concluding with boards of directors, and including several others in between.

We have been trying to solve the mystery of why ever-increasing acquisitions go ahead despite ever-increasing evidence that many yield no operating gains. We have identified incentive misalignment: even where merger brings no operating gains, it may boost pay (and other benefits) for key players including senior executives of acquirer and target, advisers, and fund managers. Also, M&A can create opportunities to extract rents (in the economist's sense: gaining wealth without increasing wealth) at the expense of stakeholders including employees and some creditors. Such rents can mean that earnings for equity-holders rise even where operating gains are negative. Then asymmetric information can create opportunities for deals which are lucrative for the buyer even if the acquisition yields zero or negative operating gains. And information problems often impede thorough scrutiny of deals *ex ante* or monitoring *ex post*.

Table 12.1 details the specific rents, information asymmetries and incentive problems we have analysed. It suggests measures that could be deployed to eliminate or mitigate these problems. And it identifies who has the authority to implement such measures—ranging, as mentioned,

© 2022 Geoff Meeks and J. Gay Meeks, CC BY-NC-ND 4.0 https://doi.org/10.11647/OBP.0309.12

from government to non-executive directors. We only suggest the general thrust of potential reforms. Designing precise mechanisms requires more expertise in law, regulation, taxation, banking and governance than we can claim.

Table 12.1 Policy responses to prevent or deter mergers which yield no socially useful operating gains.

Challenge	Response	By whom?
Rent extraction		
Moral hazard	Protection for non-equity stakeholders	Government
Tax avoidance	Remove tax break for interest	Government
	Eliminate tax privilege for capital gains	Government
	Equalise national corporation taxes	Governments
Rigged debt market	End interest rate manipulation	Central bank
Price gouging	Antitrust	Government
Asymmetric information		
Creative accounting to inflate bidder's share price	Rigorous accounting standards	Accounting regulators
Weak *ex ante* evaluation of bids	Greater and more consistent disclosure	Non-executive directors (NEDs) Accounting regulators
	Independent evaluation of proposals	Listing authorities Takeover Panel
Weak *ex post* monitoring of deal outcomes	Tighter accounting rules	Accounting regulators

Challenge	Response	By whom?
Misaligned incentives		
Fund manager short-termism	Modify contracts: defer bonuses	Institutional investors
Advisers rewarded for completing deal, not for success of deal	Modify contracts: just costs reimbursed on completion; deferred rewards based on performance outcomes	NEDs
NEDs' pay not linked to merger outcomes	Deferred pay linked to outcomes	Shareholders
Perverse incentives for top executives	No bonuses just for completion Weaken link between size and pay Deferred rewards linked to outcomes	NEDs

Curbing Rent Extraction Arising from Distorted Financial Engineering

One device for rent extraction has been an acquisition financed largely by debt (Chapter 5). Running the business with a very small equity cushion magnifies the gains for equity-holders if things go well. But it also increases the risk of bankruptcy; and limited liability provisions shift much of this downside risk onto other stakeholders—moral hazard. Chapters 5 and 11 document the resulting losses incurred by suppliers and employees, and the weak protection afforded to such groups by existing regulation.

Prima facie, the logical response to the abuse of limited liability protection for equity-holders is to reduce the protection for those responsible for decisions on how much debt to contract. Such a reform has repercussions far beyond the M&A market and is currently being debated by academics and practitioners (e.g. Goodhart and Lastra 2020).

Another approach is to strengthen the protections for vulnerable victims of moral hazard—especially unsecured creditors and pensioners. As Chapter 11 above reports, the protections currently offered in the UK have been attacked in parliamentary discussion of the Carillion failure as inadequate. The framework and institutions have existed in the UK—the Prompt Payment Code to protect suppliers, and the Pension Protection Fund for retirees—but they have proved to be weak.

The moral hazard problem is also linked to remuneration practices, as quoted earlier: 'Existing contracts that are poorly designed allow bosses of quoted companies to become rich by using leverage to game earnings per share and performance targets.' (Ford 2020a). Debt-funded acquisitions which increase risk can boost earnings per share when operating profits are unchanged (or even diminished) as a result of merger (Chapter 5). It is within the power of board remuneration committees to mitigate this distortion. Also, greater reliance on deferred remuneration (discussed below) might exert a moderating influence on the debt-equity choice: executives of the acquirer would share more of the pain if the firm failed in years following the acquisition.

Anomalies in tax systems have offered further opportunities for rent extraction in M&A (Chapter 6). In most jurisdictions the interest payable on debt is deductible when calculating corporation tax—a gift to borrowers at others' expense, and a further stimulus to morally hazardous reliance on debt. Criticism of the tax deductibility of interest payments is heard in many contexts apart from M&A.[1] We have read no compelling defence of the status quo. Removing the privilege would not be technically difficult: governments have the powers to eliminate this distortion. And similarly, the privileged tax treatment of capital gains (versus income) seems to have no basis in fairness or efficiency: M&A offers rich opportunities to convert 'income' into (privileged) 'capital gains', opportunities exploited to great effect by Private Equity (Chapter 7). Again, government has the powers to remove the bias. But they face powerful vested interests, who threaten to move their earnings to tax havens if their privileges are withdrawn.

Such threats to national governments arise from substantial differences between tax rates in different jurisdictions, the last of the

---

1   E.g. Fleischer (2020), Wolf (2021a).

tax-based distortions we highlighted in Chapter 6: 'tax inversion' using cross-border merger to redomicile a firm to a lower tax jurisdiction. This too is technically easy to eliminate by harmonising tax rates. But countries using low tax rates to attract footloose multinationals resist such proposals. The OECD and the Biden Administration in the US are supporting such reforms to prevent the international tax system from 'collapsing under the weight of its own complexity and competition in tax rates' (Devereux, in Smyth and Giles 2021).

Foroohar (2022) gives a colourful account of another opportunity to extract rents via debt-funded M&A, one provided by central banks which in recent years have 'in some profound way, manipulated the market'.[2] They have pumped 'unprecedented amounts of money into the US economy [...] [which] encourage ever more risky behaviour on Wall Street', as we illustrated with the highly leveraged acquisitions in Chapters 6 and 7. Foroohar describes the result as '[...] a dysfunctional dance in which the fortunes of asset owners versus everyone else moved further and further apart.' And her policy prescription is that 'both interest rates and balance sheets need to be normalised.'

Central banks mostly agree, and they have the tools to normalise, but face powerful resistance from the asset owners who have benefitted from the rigged interest rate, as well as from finance ministries which find artificially low interest rates helpful in meeting the interest payable on high levels of public sector debt.

Chapters 1 and 2 gave further examples of rent extraction where mergers eliminated competitors and permitted price gouging at the expense of customers and suppliers. Not only income distribution is affected—allocative efficiency is impaired when customers who would be willing to buy a product for what it costs to produce[3] (or somewhat more) are priced out of the market.

Although earlier chapters gave examples of such behaviour in the airline, pharmaceutical, and social media industries we have not explored this subject in any detail. That is not because it is considered unimportant—far from it. It is because it has already been extensively

---

2   Foroohar's comments come in a review of Leonard's (2022) study of central bank policy.

3   Including the cost of capital.

analysed by economists for many decades,[4] and we discuss it in some detail in a 'sister' publication (Meeks, Meeks and Meeks forthcoming). Historically, the first vigorous intervention to limit such rent extraction is associated particularly with US President Theodore Roosevelt early last century. In Europe, government controls on mergers which diminish competition began to be introduced from the middle of the twentieth century. In more recent years, restrictions on merger have become tighter in Europe than in the United States.

Compelling critiques of the passivity of antitrust policy in the US have been published recently. Wu reports that '[i]n the United States, between 1997 and 2012, 75% of American industries became more concentrated' (p. 21). Tepper and Hearn complain: 'Mergers that materially reduce the number of competitors should be prevented. Today, merger enforcement is dead' (p. 242). And Philippon concludes that 'many private companies have grown so dominant that they can get away with bad service, high prices, and deficient privacy safeguards. Only two decades ago, the United States was effectively the land of free markets and a leader in deregulation and antitrust policy. It must remember its own history and relearn the lessons it successfully taught the rest of the world' (p. 288).[5]

---

4   It is also difficult to explore this process fully with the accounting model and data we have available and deploy in Chapter 1 and Appendix 1. The accounting data for operating profit in company reports include gains from increased efficiency, better products/services, etc., along with the rents from price gouging. An improvement in operating profit may reflect more efficient operations, or the exercise of monopolistic or monopsonistic power. However, because market power rarely diminishes as a result of merger, we can generally be confident that a decline in reported operating profit (the outcome often observed—see Appendix 1) signals diminished efficiency.

5   The case for tougher antitrust goes beyond the concerns about rent extraction which relate to our main mystery theme—why mergers which yield no operating gains proceed with increasing frequency. It has been argued that deals which yield operating efficiencies may still be contrary to the public interest. One reason has been that some M&A is associated with concentration of political—not just market—power, which in turn entrenches the inequality of income and wealth (Meeks, Meeks and Meeks forthcoming). Another is that cross-border mergers may threaten national security: such concerns led Norway to block the sale of Bergen Engines to TMH, a buyer from Russia, which was seen as a military rival (Pfeifer and Milne 2021).

A broader concept of national interest lay behind the call for a ban on the proposed purchase of the UK's Arm Holdings by US Nvidia. Critics of the deal emphasised the central role of Arm in the UK's IT ecosystem, and the public funding of research and education which underpinned its success. And they contended that Nvidia's previous acquisition of a UK tech business ended in the UK operation being closed,

Reducing Information Asymmetry

Deficiencies of information impinge on M&A in several ways. When insider managers have better information than outsider shareholders, incentives can arise for acquisitions funded by share exchange which yield no operating gains: 'acquisitions are made by overvalued acquirers of relatively less overvalued targets' (Shleifer and Vishny 2003, as quoted in Chapter 8). Then, as well as taking advantage of opportunities created by asymmetric information, firms may manage information so as to create such opportunities—there is a 'powerful incentive to get their equity overvalued, so that they can make acquisitions with shares'. Chapter 9 and Appendix 2 explain the creative accounting techniques which have been available in recent decades to achieve such overvaluation.

Chapter 3 recounted criticisms of the limited amount and reliability of information provided to non-executive directors (and sometimes shareholders) about the prospective gains from an acquisition. This is a matter of concern to the International Accounting Standards Board (IASB 2020). For some deals in the UK the Listing Authority and the Takeover Panel demand the provision of some forward-looking data. But, although assembled typically by advisers, these are ultimately the responsibility of management, whose interest may lie in presenting a flattering picture of prospective gains (research shows that their projections have typically been over-optimistic (Chapter 9)).[6] In Chapter 3 we noted the expert advice given to the parliamentary 'inquest' on RBS: 'it should be the norm that independent advice is taken, which is

---

the staff fired, and the HQ and IP being shipped abroad (Hauser 2020). This bid may be diminishing the efficiency of ARM. The 2020 proposal was eventually abandoned in February 2022 after opposition from the antitrust authorities in spring 2022. Hill (2019 and 2022) discusses the efficiency losses when targets are left in limbo for long periods while bids are unresolved.

In the UK at the time of writing, a National Security and Investment Bill is under consideration which 'will take a more intrusive approach to foreign takeovers' (Pickard, Bradshaw and Thomas 2021). This is targeted at tech industries. There have been 'only 12 public interest interventions by the government on national security grounds since 2002'.

6   Scrutiny and verification of forecasts would be aided by a framework for disclosures and measurement specified by standard-setters. We recognise, of course, that specifying a particular measure invites manipulation (Chapter 9).

not remunerated on the basis of success with the transaction'[7] (where 'success' means simply completing the transaction, the current basis for advisers' success fees, not completing a *profitable* transaction—see below).

Information problems intrude at other stages of the bid and acquisition process. Earnings management ahead of bids can mislead the market, distort the prices of acquirers' own shares used to pay for targets, and lead to self-serving mergers which might otherwise not proceed. Then accounting for the integration of acquirees offers rich opportunities to flatter performance measures which influence executive pay and share prices, and facilitate further acquisitions. Accounting standard-setters have been energetic in foiling such techniques, but new ones are always being invented. The UK's arch critic of creative accounting, Terry Smith (1996), after praising the achievements of the UK's Accounting Standards Board in eradicating many creative accounting devices, commented that standard-setting is 'a bit like painting the Forth Bridge. Once it is finished you start all over again [...] whatever rules you put in place, smart people will find a way to express a distorted or flattering picture of their performance'(p. 10).

Accounting procedures after merger could more effectively hold executives to account for their spending on acquisitions. Accounting standard-setters proposed measures to achieve this late last century: compulsory charges against profit to amortise the goodwill representing the vast sums expended on acquisitions over and above the fair value of the separable assets that came with the target. But in the US, and then international, standards these proposals were thwarted by executives' lobbying (Chapter 9 and Appendix 2). Impairment tests were adopted instead but proved to be vulnerable to manipulation (Appendix 2). At the time of writing, the US Financial Accounting Standards Board is minded to revert to amortisation (Lugo 2020), and the International Accounting Standards Board has the subject under review (IASB 2020).[8]

---

7   Sir David Walker (in HoC 2012). Such independent assessment—free of management bias and advisers' conflict of interest—could also be part of the information provided to shareholders in those cases where the Takeover Panel or the Listing Authority mandate such disclosures.

8   Reverting to amortisation could have a further benefit for efficiency—mitigating the intangibles anomaly outlined in Chapter 9, whereby generating some intangible

Better Aligning Incentives

Chapters 2 to 4 identified four key players in M&A who often have strong incentives (or weak disincentives) to support a deal even if it brings no operating gains: the bidder's CEO; the CEO's immediate 'supervisors'— the non-executive directors; the directors' advisers (investment bankers and other professionals); and the managers of funds which own shares in the target.[9] In each case contracts could be redesigned to eliminate or weaken incentives to complete an unpromising merger, and strengthen incentives to support those which promise operating gains.

'If you are a fund manager holding an investment that attracts a bid at a 40 per cent premium, you'll vote to take it', observed Somerset-Webb (2017). 'Can't be bad for the performance numbers on which your bonus is based, can it? [...] Pointing out that short-termism in investment as a problem is not exactly new'. A major pensions provider has made a general argument against bonuses based on performance fees: 'Scottish Widows sees no evidence to suggest that performance fees improve customer outcomes' (Cumbo and Wiggins 2021). Eliminating them would weaken the perverse incentive to opt for the premium offered by the bidder now when retaining shares in the target would be in the shareholder's long-term interest.

As for the acquirer's advisers, we already noted the expert's recommendation in the parliamentary report on the failure of RBS after its acquisition of a large segment of ABN/AMRO: an independent assessment of the bid proposal should be made available to the board (and where appropriate to shareholders); and the advisers completing that assessment should not have a financial interest in the bid going ahead. Where different advisers were employed to help execute the deal, a conventional contracting device to align their interest with the acquirer shareholders' interests would be to defer any 'success fee', linking it to the post-merger performance of the acquirer.[10]

A similar prescription was offered at the parliamentary hearing for non-executive directors of the acquirer:

---

assets internally can lead to lower reported profits than buying them in an acquisition.

9   And the acquirer's shares in cases where the acquirer's shareholders have a say, such as class 1 deals by listed companies in the UK.

10   Paying the cost of the advice in the meantime.

there is a strong case for more substantial deferment of pay. I would include in that non-executive directors, so that related to some performance measure their fee [...] is not available to them, or in some part not available to them, for three or four years, by which time the company will have demonstrated success or failure.[11]

Replacing the NED's fixed salary with such an arrangement might encourage him to scrutinise prospective bids more critically, and take independent advice, rather than—as one NED we quoted in Chapter 4 put it—see his (highly paid) role at the board as just being to 'applaud' the CEO.

Two items of evidence about M&A that we emphasised in Chapters 1 and 2 were McKinsey's estimate that '70% fail', and Harford and Li's finding that 'even in mergers where bidding shareholders are worse off, bidding CEOs are better off three quarters of the time'. It is surely bizarre that in these circumstances some NEDs award large bonuses to executives just for carrying out an acquisition. It is not so bizarre that executives are frequently awarded a permanent rise in base salary for the increase in firm size resulting from M&A: the argument is that they carry heavier responsibilities (more employees to supervise, more assets to protect). But Chapter 2 discussed suggestions that M&A actually often lightened the burden of running the acquirer: it could secure a quieter life by eliminating challengers, and make the acquirer less vulnerable to becoming a target itself.

Greater reliance on deferred pay which is contingent on post-merger performance is likely to encourage fewer mergers that fail to produce operating gains—all the more so if accompanied by some of the measures outlined above to reduce rent extraction, and to limit the opportunities for executives to manipulate performance measures.

The list of proposed measures in Table 12.1 is diverse and daunting. But in a market with expenditure of several billion dollars a year the potential gains from even modest improvements in efficiency can be considerable. And the correctives suggested could also mitigate some of the highly regressive impacts of merger on income distribution—only touched on in this book, but explored in our forthcoming study, *Rising Inequality: The Contribution of Corporate Merger*. A wide range of measures

---

11   Sir David Walker in HoC 2012, para 88.

is needed because we are dealing with, as Phalippou put it, 'a complex environment riddled with multiple layers of agency conflicts' where 'misleading information does proliferate' (see Chapter 7). A central message of our book is that misaligned incentives, distorted financial engineering, and asymmetric information interact and cumulate to produce a dysfunctional market. But this is not to say that progress on a single front among these would not be worthwhile in its own right, as a partial advance. Equally, although our analysis indicates that the suggested measures taken together and well implemented give the prospect of significantly increasing efficiency in this market, still they may fall short of providing a complete remedy. For chief executives, for instance, some psychological enticements to undertake mergers that fail to yield operating gains might remain even if the major lure of winning enhanced pay is effectively constrained. As Collins (in Chapter 2) summed up the combination of inducements:

> Think of the impact of a 'transformational' deal, the thrill of the chase, the media spotlight, the boasting rights and—of course—the massive pay rises. You will be number one! [...] By the time it all ends in tears, the executives who have laid waste to the shareholders are long departed *with their winnings*. [emphasis added]

Appendix 1:
Measuring Success or Failure

Chapter 1 used a standard accounting framework to identify potential sources of gain from merger. For the acquirer's shareholders these included:

   A. higher prices because the merger leads to improved products or services

   B. higher prices because the merger leads to increased monopolistic power

   C. lower costs because of net synergies—e.g. economies of scale

   D. lower costs because the merger leads to increased monopsonistic power

But part or all of these gains will be partly offset by:

   E. extra pay for executives

   F. merger transaction costs, including advisers' fees

The sum of items A to F will appear in the change in operating profit, P. The acquirer's shareholders may also gain from merger because of:

   G. borrowing to fund the merger on terms made favourable by limited liability

   H. privileged tax treatment of borrowing, capital gains, etc.

The overall private merger gains to the acquirer's shareholders will then appear in earnings, Q, operating profit minus interest and tax.

   From a social—whole economy—point of view, B, D, G and H are just transfers from other interest groups and don't represent any gain to the

© 2022 Geoff Meeks and J. Gay Meeks, CC BY-NC-ND 4.0 https://doi.org/10.11647/OBP.0309.13

economy. Also, a social calculus would include a cost not represented in the firm's accounts:

I.   consumer surplus, the loss to customers priced out of the market.

In general, of the readily available measures, P comes closest to reflecting the social, economy-wide gains from merger, although it will typically be upward-biased, overstating the social gains. This is because it includes the gains at customers' and suppliers' expense arising from the merged firm's increased market power. And it excludes losses of consumer surplus. Q is further upward-biased as a measure of social gains because it includes benefits at others' expense arising from limited liability and tax privileges.

Many of the studies of merger success have been concerned just with the shareholders' interests. Such accounting studies have focused on measures based on Q (earnings). An alternative approach—feasible only for companies listed on a stock exchange—has instead deployed a measure R, related to Q. R comprises share price appreciation plus dividends: how much a shareholder gains if she buys a share at the beginning of the year, receives dividends during the year and sells the share at the end of the year. Over time, R is expected to be closely linked to Q: current dividends appear in both measures, and share price appreciation reflects expectations of future dividends.

Research in the finance literature has largely been based on R—a shareholder perspective; in the accounting literature on P and Q; and in the industrial organisation literature on P—a societal perspective (though, as explained above, typically an upward-biased measure of social gains).

Time Frames

Accounts-based studies typically compare P or Q achieved in the years following merger with the corresponding numbers achieved by the participants before they combined. Studies employing share prices follow two different approaches. One, the event study, reports R in the weeks leading up to the deal announcement and completion—on the argument that the stock market will impound in share prices the earnings gains expected after the merger. The other, longer-run approach traces R over the years surrounding the merger. The event studies have tended to record more successes than the long-run ones, prompting Jensen and Ruback (1983) to comment:

> these post-outcome negative abnormal returns are unsettling because they are inconsistent with market efficiency and suggest that changes in stock prices during takeovers overestimate the future efficiency gains from merger. (p. 20)

Chapter 8 above discussed such issues around market efficiency.

Caves (1989) pointed out a similar divergence between stock market event studies and longer-run accounting analyses. The former report 'a bundle for the target's shareholders plus zero for the bidder's [...] supporting the conclusion that mergers create value and accordingly are economically efficient'; whilst recent accounting studies 'are resoundingly negative on the average productivity of merger and sharply at variance with the findings of the event studies' (pp. 153, 158).

And this contrast between *ex ante* and *ex post* assessments is congruent with comparisons of managers' forecasts of post-merger earnings with the actual out-turns—discussed in Chapter 9.

Another strand of performance measurement, pioneered by Healy et al. (1992), develops a hybrid measure, mixing accounting data with stock market data. An income measure from the accounts is used in the numerator, and a stock market measure of the firm's assets is used as the denominator. If—as Jensen and Ruback commented above—share prices typically decline after merger ('post outcome negative abnormal returns'), unchanged accounting income will translate into an improvement in the value of the ratio, simply because the denominator is shrinking. Amel-Zadeh (2020) explores and illustrates in detail the biases in such measures. Because of the potential biases we have not included these studies in Table A.1.[1] The majority of them report a positive result for post-merger returns.

---

1   Such studies (some negative, more positive) include, in date order, Healy et al. (1992), Cornett and Tehranian (1992), Switzer (1996), Harford (1999), Ghosh (2001), Linn and Switzer (2001), Megginson et al. (2004), Powell and Stark (2005). Healy et al. is included in Table A.1.

Acquirer and Target

A convenient feature of the event studies is that they are able to distinguish the gains for the acquirer's shareholders from those for the target's. Stock market data are available for the target up to the moment it is acquired. For example, Moeller et al. (2005) were able to conclude that, although target firm shareholders gained, 'the losses of bidders exceed the gains by targets [...] by $134 billion'.

Mostly, neither of the long-run measures—using R or P—is able to distinguish the contribution of the target to the amalgamation's results after merger. One exception for R was in China, where acquired companies retained separate stock market listings after merger (Song and Meeks 2020). And an exception for P was possible for Ravenscraft and Scherer (1987) who analysed lines of business data which were collected by government for a limited period. They concluded:

> [...] one third of all acquisitions were subsequently sold off [...] On average merged lines later sold off had a negative operating income during the last year before they were resold. Among the survivors, profitability also tended to decline...

Other Things Equal

It goes without saying that no serious study is based on the raw accounting or share price data. Gains are measured relative to benchmarks: matched samples or peer groups, so that industry-wide or stock market-wide fluctuations in performance are not attributed to merger.

And the data are scaled—expressed in ratio form: profits to assets, stock market returns relative to initial stock market value of the business.

Examples

Table A.1 lists peer-reviewed studies of the impact of merger on performance published in the last half-century. Although it includes over fifty works, it is not comprehensive. The members of the list are drawn largely from reviews/surveys by various writers of the academic literatures of accounting, economics and finance. These will have missed some work in these and related areas, but we see no reason to fear any selection bias.

One valuable related strand of literature not included in Table A.1 explores whether particular subsets of deals achieve better results than others. These studies include Chatterjee and Meeks (1996), Healy et al. (1997), Rau and Vermaelen (1998), Capron (1999), Capron and Pistre (2002), and Gregory (2005).

Obviously it is impossible to do justice in the table to the rich analyses and nuances and caveats in these many thousands of published pages. Further discussion of measurement methods can be found in Caves (1989), Chatterjee and Meeks (1996), Conn et al. (1985), Healy et al. (1992), Jensen and Ruback (1983), Scherer (1988), and the chapters by Meeks and Meeks, Amel-Zadeh, and Song and Meeks in Amel-Zadeh and Meeks (2020).

As well as reporting for each study listed in Table A.1 the publication date and the country (if it is not the US), we note the type of data used (stock market returns unless otherwise specified). The final column marks as positive those studies which report clear gains for the acquirer—eleven of the fifty-five. Note our contention above that measures based on P are likely to overstate overall gains to the economy, Q and R even more so.

Table A.1 Statistical studies of the impact of M&A on performance.

Author(s)	Pub'n Date	Country note 1	Data note 2	Impact note 3
Singh	1971	UK	Acc	
Lev/Mandelker	1972		Acc	
Ryden	1972	Sweden		positive
Mandelker	1974			
Utton	1974	UK	Acc	
Meeks	1977	UK	Acc	
Langetieg	1978			
Firth	1979	UK		
Cable et al.	1980	Germany	Acc	
Cosh et al.	1980	UK	Acc	positive

Author(s)	Pub'n	Country	Data	Impact
Dodd	1980			
Firth	1980	UK		
Kumps et al.	1980	Belgium	Acc	
Jenny/Weber	1980	France	Acc	
Peer	1980	Netherlands	Acc	
Ryden/Edberg	1980	Sweden	Acc	
Mueller	1980		Acc	
Asquith/Kim	1982			
Asquith	1983			
Malatesta	1983			
Eckbo	1983			
Asquith et al.	1983			positive
Kumar	1984	UK	Acc	
Dennis/McConnell	1986			
Ravenscraft/Scherer	1987		Acc	
Bradley et al.	1988			positive
Franks/Harris	1989	UK		positive
Lahey/Conn	1990			
Limmack	1991	UK		
Agrawal et al.	1992			
Healy et al.	1992		Acc	positive
Dickerson et al.	1997	UK	Acc	
Gregory	1997	UK		
Loughran/Vijh	1997			
Dickerson et al.	2000	UK	Acc	
Andrade et al.	2001			positive
Desbriere/Schatt	2002	France	Acc	positive
Sudarsanam/Mahate	2003			
Diaz et al.	2004	Europe	Acc	positive
Andre et al.	2004	Canada		
Moeller et al.	2005			
Rahman/Limmack	2004	Malaysia	Acc	positive
Knapp et al.	2005		Acc	
Guest et al.	2010	UK		

Author(s)	Pub'n	Country	Data	Impact
Gu/Lev	2011			
Duchin/Schmidt	2013			
Zhou et al.	2015	China		positive
Dargenidou et al.	2016	UK		
Ma et al.	2016	China	Acc	
Boateng et al.	2017	China	Acc	
Cuypers et al.	2017			
Malmendier et al.	2018			
Amel-Zadeh	2020		Acc	
Amel-Zadeh/Meeks	2020			
Song/Meeks	2020	China		

Notes: See the discussion in Appendix 1 of contributions to this literature not included in this table. See the reference list for full publication details. 1. US unless otherwise specified. 2. Stock market data unless otherwise specified (Acc = company accounts). 3. Positive if clear gains, consistent across measures (impact relates to acquirer where target also studied).

Appendix II:
Managing Earnings around M&A

In this appendix we provide more detail, illustration and interpretation of some of the creative accounting devices deployed in connection with M&A and discussed in Chapters 9 and 10.

Ahead of an Offer

The main thrust of creative accounting at this stage is to flatter current performance by bringing profit forward from future accounting periods. The aim is thereby to secure a higher share price than would otherwise be warranted, and to use the bidder's own shares as payment for the target (Shleifer and Vishny 2003). A similar strategy has been observed ahead of other major financial transactions such as seasoned equity offerings unrelated to M&A (Rangan 1998). A symmetric strategy—managing earnings downwards so that the managers secure a more favourable deal with the owners—has been observed ahead of management buyouts (Perry and Williams 1994). If successful, the profit enhancement strategy brings a once-and-for-all financial gain to the acquirers: they secure the deal on more favourable terms. In the absence of such major transactions, earnings management would produce only temporary gains in share price, which would be reversed in future periods. Such shifting of profit between periods could, however, still be favoured for other reasons—for example, to smooth earnings or to take advantage of the terms of a performance-related pay contract, timing the earnings for when they would generate the biggest bonuses (Chapter 2).

The illustrations we give come from the US and the UK. They span different regulatory regimes, and some have since been outlawed by the accounting regulators. They do not all relate directly to M&A

© 2022 Geoff Meeks and J. Gay Meeks, CC BY-NC-ND 4.0
https://doi.org/10.11647/OBP.0309.14

strategies—they are chosen because they are well documented, and undisputed, and help illustrate the mechanisms of creative accounting. As Chapter 9 explained, many cases of creative accounting cannot be proved without access to detailed internal information.

1.Delaying Recognition of Costs of Multi-year Contracts

Opportunities for such manipulation arise in the common case where a fixed price is charged for delivering products or services over several years, and the future costs of delivery are inevitably uncertain. In the early years of the contract executives have to take a view on the distribution of costs—and therefore of profits—over the lifetime of the contract. Profits can be front-loaded by end-loading the costs. One such opportunity was exploited by Xerox. They supplied office equipment through leases which charged an annual fee covering both the initial capital cost of the equipment, and provision of servicing through its lifetime, and a finance charge for the capital outlay. The SEC (2002a) alleged that creative accounting "accelerated Xerox's recognition of equipment revenue by over \$3billion and increased its pre-tax earnings by approx. \$1.5billion over the four-year period from 1997 through 2000". The manipulation added in the most affected quarter some 50% to earnings per share—at a time when Xerox made "four offerings that registered nearly \$9billion worth of debt securities" (SEC 2002a). Xerox paid a \$10 million fine to the SEC, "but without admitting or denying the allegations in the complaint" (SEC 2002b). Because the manipulation was buried in the unreported calculations underlying the published accounts, it is unlikely that outside investors would have been able to see through and reverse out the earnings management.[1] The offerings were not directly related to acquisitions, though Xerox did acquire Tektronix in 2000 for towards a billion dollars.

Then Gryta and Mann (2020) give an example for the Power division of serial acquirer GE:

---

[1] These are intended only as illustrations of the opportunities for earnings manipulation. Others, including the manipulation of inventory valuations, provisions for bad and doubtful debts, sale and repurchase and sale and leaseback, are discussed in Jones (2011), Mulford and Comiskey (2005), Sherman et al. (2003), Schilit and Perler (2010), Smith (1992, 1996), and Tweedie, Cook and Whittington (forthcoming).

To GE investors, Power seemed to have been making its numbers and putting up solid profits. But those were illusory. The accounting tricks that looked like profits were actually just borrowing from the company's future earnings to cover up problems in the present.

Power had sold service guarantees to many of its customers that extended out for decades. By tweaking its estimate of the future cost of fulfilling those contracts, it could report boosts to profit as needed. [...] In this period, GE was acquiring about four businesses a month. (Gryta and Mann, pp. 7, 17).

In the UK, a parliamentary committee investigated the record of the serial acquirer, Carillion, after it failed (Carillion is discussed at length in Chapter 11). Shortly before its failure a reappraisal of the prospective costs relating to long-term construction contracts led it to 'reduce the value of several major contracts by a total of £845 million'. Soon after, '£200 million extra was added, completely wiping out the company's last seven years of profits' and leaving it insolvent (net liabilities of £405 million) (HoC 2018, p. 79)

The difficulty for an outsider to see through such disparities in earnings is illustrated by the fact that the company had in the preceding years of these contracts received unqualified audit reports from Big 4 auditors KPMG, who had access to internal records and the company's staff. But as one of Carillion's principal investors commented, 'changes of this magnitude do not generally materialize "overnight"' (HoC, p. 81)

2.Accelerating Sales and Profits

Sherman et al. (2003) give several examples of companies using opaque devices which bring forward or front-load earnings. In one of these, Coca Cola used a 'channel stuffing' device: they persuaded local bottler-franchisees to take delivery of concentrate, ahead of when it was needed, achieving the bottlers' cooperation by paying the storage costs and deferring the payment date until the time when the product would normally have been delivered. The shipment would be included in Coca Cola's sales and would swell its profit in the earlier period.

3.Deferring Interest Charges

In the last century, banks in the UK developed a rash of complex financial instruments which deferred interest payments on company borrowing—and the charges in the profit and loss account, thereby bringing forward reported (post-interest) earnings. These included stepped interest bonds, deep discount bonds, and convertible loan stock with premium puts (Tweedie et al. forthcoming). These instruments were widely used in a period of intensive merger activity until the Accounting Standards Board's's FRS4 required the finance costs associated with such liabilities to be allocated to accounting periods at a constant rate irrespective of the structure of the cash payments stipulated by the instrument (Tweedie et al. forthcoming).

4. Rescheduling Profits by Manipulating the Valuation of Assets and Liabilities on the Balance Sheet

Assigning a value to some components of the balance sheet requires assumptions and forecasts. And the executives are typically best-informed to make those assumptions and forecasts. A change in the value assigned to an asset or liability will generally translate into a change in profit. The creative accountant has to adopt a different strategy over such valuations depending on the stage of the acquisition process. Ahead of a deal (in particular a share for share deal) the creative accountant will typically want to overstate assets and understate liabilities, to give a short-term, pre-bid boost to profits and the share price. But when integrating the target upon acquisition, the creative accountant will face opportunities to flatter post-merger profits by understating some of the acquired assets and overstating provisions triggered by the acquisition.

In relation to inventory, accounting rules generally require valuation as the lower of cost or net realisable value (NRV). NRV may fall below cost when, for example, the inventory is perishable (e.g. fish), out of fashion (e.g. clothing), or obsolescent (e.g. tech products). Auditors will look to executives to assess such deterioration; and in examples we cite below the discretion afforded to executives amounted to $290 m in one year at Cisco (Sherman et al. 2003), and £334 million at Guinness (Paterson 1988).

When businesses are assessing how much of the money owed to them by customers (or by banks' borrowers) will be repaid in full, they have to take a view on how much they will recover from customers they know are bankrupt, and how many debtors who appear healthy might become financially distressed before they have paid outstanding amounts.

A whistleblower from inside Tesco led to the company being accused by the Financial Conduct Authority of improper overstatement of receivables in the form of rebates expected from suppliers, thereby inflating profit by £326 million (Felsted and Agnew 2014). Tesco paid £215 million in a fine, and compensation to investors who had been misled. However, Tesco used a "Deferred Prosecution Agreement (DPA)", which does not require an admission of wrongdoing.

Understating payables similarly brings a short-term profit gain. And Tesco was accused by the UK Groceries Code Adjudicator of understating payables, having unilaterally withheld full payment to suppliers (Ram 2016; Vandevelde and Thomas 2016). In this case, Tesco faced no financial penalty as the misconduct predated the Adjudicator's power to impose fines.

Accounting for the Deal

When it comes to recording the impact of the deal on the acquirer's accounts, creative accountants have for the last many decades been preoccupied with 'purchased goodwill'. Purchased goodwill is a nebulous, transient sort of asset—a residual, calculated as the difference between the purchase consideration for an acquired business and the fair value of its separable assets. It is rationalised as an entitlement to future profits arising from the merger.

The sums involved are material, and growing. If we think of the price paid for a target, it will typically exceed the accounting book value of the target's assets for two reasons. First, the market price of the target's share before a deal is contemplated has typically been of the order of 160% of the book value of the target's assets (Penman and Reggiani 2014)—albeit varying a good deal from firm to firm and year to year. Then the acquirer typically has to pay a substantial premium over the previous share price to gain acceptance of a bid by the majority of the target's shareholders—of the order of 30% (Amel-Zadeh and Meeks 2019). So if the acquirer integrates the individual target assets at their book value, there will be a significant residual to be allocated to goodwill. Where the target has relied heavily on internally generated intangible assets which—following accounting rules—have not been recorded in its balance sheet, the acquisition will lead to especially significant goodwill in the acquirer's balance sheet. For example, when Vodafone paid £101 billion for Mannesmann, purchased goodwill represented £83 billion of the total. Likewise, purchased goodwill was the major component of HP's purchase of Autonomy and SoftBank's acquisition of Arm. And purchased goodwill has become ever more important for the company sector for two reasons. First, as we reported in Chapter 1, expenditure on M&A globally has grown vigorously: in the West, in aggregate it has overtaken CAPEX—investment in new tangibles (Mauboussin and Callahan 2014, 2015). And, second, business spending on intangibles has grown much faster than investment in tangible assets over recent decades (Corrado and Hutton 2010, Srivastava 2014)—think of Apple, Facebook, and Microsoft...

When shareholders' funds are used to buy tangible assets with finite lives—such as machines, aircraft, vehicles and computers—the initial outlay is charged to the Profit and Loss Account (P&L)—as depreciation—over the lifetime of the asset. This keeps a check on whether the executives' spending on the assets has been recouped through subsequent revenue—whether the executives have been effective stewards of the investors' funds. At times, the accounting standard-setters have required that an analogous annual charge—amortisation of a portion of the cost—be made to the P&L to write down the cost of goodwill over its lifetime. Such charges can make a huge difference to the bottom line of the P&L—think of Vodafone's £83 billion of goodwill (above). And acquirers' executives have made extraordinary efforts to avoid amortisation of this goodwill—with the corresponding hit to profits.

By late last century the national accounting standard-setters in the UK and US had determined to clamp down on devices allowing executives to obscure spending on goodwill and thus avoid amortisation. The UK's innovative ASB required in almost all cases that the goodwill appear in the balance sheet with its depletion recorded via amortisation in the

P&L (supplemented by impairment—discretionary write-downs—if amortisation did not keep pace with the depletion of goodwill). The Financial Accounting Standards Board (FASB) in the US proposed similar arrangements.

However, FASB's proposal triggered a fierce counter-attack by American executives and their lobbyists (see Beresford 2001, Zeff 2002). One Cisco executive even protested to a Senate hearing that the proposed accounting would 'stifle technology development, impede capital formation and slow job creation'.[2] Accountants had never realised they were so powerful!

FASB backed down. They abandoned amortisation and left it to executives to decide on any impairment.

When, soon afterwards, the International Accounting Standards Board (IASB), the international standard-setter, was formed, its American members had no appetite to re-open this dispute, and the US impairment-only regime was adopted for international standards. When UK listed companies became governed by IASB standards from 2005, amortisation was ruled out for them too.[3]

This reform actually turned out to provide a great opportunity for creative accountants. It created opportunities to construct the combination's accounts so that strong profits could be reported after merger even if the merger failed in the sense of reducing underlying operating profits.

Before then, another device had been available to avoid amortisation. This presented acquisitions as mergers of equals ('pooling' or 'merger' accounting), where the purchase consideration never appeared in the accounts. This avoided any goodwill amortisation in the P&L. In one such deal, the bidder, AT&T, was prepared to expend as much as $500 million of its shareholders' funds just to have the transaction classified and accounted for without goodwill amortisation (Lys and Vincent 1995). Then Tweedie and Whittington (2020) report that the finance director of BP actually told the press that avoiding amortisation through pooling was an advantage of its acquisition of Amoco. Li (2007) estimates in this case that, had the combination instead been reported

---

2   Dennis Powell, quoted in Beresford (2001).
3   By 2020 FASB were minded to reintroduce the amortisation of goodwill (Lugo 2020).

as an acquisition, accompanied by amortisation, the amalgamation's earnings would have been reduced by percentages ranging from 8% to 37% in subsequent years. Another contrivance (common in the UK) wrote off the purchased goodwill immediately against reserves, thereby avoiding the need for any amortisation of goodwill and damage to the profit and loss account (Griffiths 1987). Wild (1987) gives the example of Saatchi and Saatchi who in 1985 wrote off £177 million of goodwill; the total capital and reserves left after the write-down was only £73 million.

Under current arrangements, if the target's inventory is marked down (automatically increasing the residual, purchased goodwill), the acquirer's cost of sales in future years (which will include items drawn from the devalued inventory) will be reduced, and reported earnings increased. Guinness were able by this device to stow up to £344 million in the cookie jar (Paterson 1988). The malleability of inventory valuation is suggested by Cisco, who wrote off inventory of $2.2 billion in 2001 (with their auditors' approval) but in the following year were able to sell $290 million of that inventory which they had shortly before valued at zero (Sherman et al. 2003). Then if the value of the target's fixed assets such as plant and machinery is marked down, future depreciation charges in the P&L will be reduced, so that reported earnings are higher. Tiphook boosted profits for the following nine years by this device, (Smith 1992, p. 27). In addition, acquirers have sometimes created a provision or reserve for future costs of reorganising the target, thereby swelling reported profits in future years. In the UK, Coloroll's cookie jar inflated reported profits more than ten-fold by this means, and in the US, Symbol Technologies created up to $186 m, and WorldCom substantial amounts (Mulford and Comiskey 2011, p. 422; Schillit and Perler 2010, p. 186). But the freedom to use this last device was drastically curtailed by the ASB in the 1990s (Tweedie, Cook and Whittington forthcoming).

Accounting Post-merger

Freed from the requirement to amortise goodwill purchased in the course of M&A, companies have had to decide whether, and by how much, to make an impairment charge in the P&L. Evidence on the unreliability and malleability of goodwill impairments has come from three sources: analysis of relevant disclosures in financial statements (e.g. Comiskey and Mulford 2010, henceforth CM); surveying or interviewing preparers, auditors and standard-setters (e.g. EFRAG/ ASBJ/OIC 2014, henceforth ASBJ; and KPMG 2014); and econometric analysis (e.g. Ramanna and Watts 2012, henceforth RW).

Several themes emerge from all three approaches. First, because goodwill consists of 'a present-value estimate of future rents' (RW, p. 755), executives' judgements are inevitably needed when selecting a valuation model, estimating future cash flows and choosing discount rates (CM). 'The subjectivity inherent in estimating goodwill's current fair value is greater than in most other asset classes such as accounts receivables, inventories and plant, making the goodwill impairment test under SFAS 142 particularly unreliable' (RW, p. 750). Auditors or board members find it difficult to challenge management's assumptions or 'to disprove them conclusively even when the assumptions seemed unduly optimistic or were not supported by historical performance' (ASBJ). Ramanna and Watts (2012) discuss the difficulty of disentangling the cash flows attributable to internally generated intangibles from those generated by the purchased goodwill. And they describe allocation procedures open to management, which can delay or accelerate impairment depending on managers' own interests.

Delay might be prompted by managers' wish to avoid or postpone reputational loss or to protect their incomes when their bonus schemes are driven by accounting profits (Elliott and Shaw 1988; Segal 2003; *Economist* 2013). Murphy (1999) reported that accounting-based compensation was usually paid out as a cash bonus, and the accounting-based compensation contracts are usually written on net income (and so include the effect of goodwill write-offs). In some circumstances, managers may have an interest instead in bringing forward or exaggerating impairments. Large impairments sometimes accompany the departure of the CEO who initiated an acquisition (this was observed following the disappointing Vodafone/Mannesmann and HP/Autonomy acquisitions, with goodwill impairments of £23.5 bn in 2006 and $9 bn in 2012 respectively). Such a 'big bath' has the advantage for the incoming CEO of 'disposing of an unwanted debit'(Arnold et al. 1992) at the expense of profit on her predecessor's watch, obviating future impairment charges and setting a low earnings base against which her subsequent performance will be judged.

These problems are recognised in the practitioner literature. '[I]t is impossible for management to have an unbiased view' (KPMG 2014, p. 8): 'management may have incentives to delay (or accelerate) or to minimise (or maximise) an impairment charge for reputational, compensation or financing covenant reasons' (KPMG 2014, p. 5). Hans Hoogervorst, Chairman of IASB, described the biases: 'in practice, entities may be hesitant to impair goodwill, so as to avoid giving the impression that they made a bad investment decision. Newly appointed CEOs, on the other hand, have a strong incentive to recognise hefty impairments on their predecessor's acquisitions' (KPMG 2014, p. 5).

RW test this agency theory prediction—that 'managers (all else equal) will, on average, use the unverifiability in goodwill accounting rules to manage financial reports opportunistically', against the view underpinning the impairment-only policy, that 'the fair value estimates [of goodwill] will, on average, allow managers to convey private information on future cash flows'. They find no evidence to confirm the latter proposition, but 'evidence of managers, on average, using the unverifiable discretion in SFAS to avoid timely goodwill disclosures where they have agency-based motives for doing so' (RW, p. 777). Amel-Zadeh, Faasse, Li and Meeks (2020) argue on the basis of a statistical study for the UK that the UK's (amortisation plus occasional impairment) regime around the millennium secured value-relevant reporting while mitigating the agency/stewardship problems associated with the current impairment-only regimes of FASB and IASB.

A Step Too Far: Accounting for Merger to Conceal a Management Failure

This accounting manipulation differs from the rest in this appendix. First, rather than often preceding failure, this one follows a failure and is designed to conceal that failure (in which it succeeded for some twenty years). Second, it fell foul of the law, something the accomplished creative accountant would never do. This case is Olympus, and is explained in a valuable *mea culpa* report published by Olympus itself (see Olympus Corporation 2011).

The origin of the problem at Olympus was that the managers had embarked on speculative investments which by 1990 had accumulated losses of some ¥100 billion. At that time these losses were not disclosed in the company's financial statements, because the assets concerned were recorded at cost, consistent with the prevailing accounting conventions. But the accounting regulations were about to change to require disclosure of the investments at "fair value"—what they were worth currently on the market.

To avoid disclosure of the latent losses, an elaborate device was created. Off balance sheet vehicles were created (in offshore jurisdictions) to buy these eroded speculative assets from the company—at their original cost. So no loss was recognised in Olympus's books. The off-balance sheet vehicles were financed by banks whose loans were in turn funded by "back-to-back" deposits from Olympus.

In due course a device was needed to deal with the latent losses embedded in the off-balance sheet vehicles, and to repay the banks. So the off-balance sheet vehicles acquired companies at fair value which were then in turn taken over by Olympus, *at inflated prices*. The inflated prices generated surpluses in the off-balance sheet vehicles, sufficient to offset the latent losses on the speculative assets which they had received from Olympus and to allow these vehicles to repay the loans with which they were financed.

At this point, Olympus held taken-over companies valued in their books at the inflated prices which had been paid to the off-balance sheet vehicles. In accordance with accounting regulations, the separable, generally tangible, assets of the new subsidiaries were recorded at fair value, and the excess of the purchase price of the acquired company over the fair value of the separable assets was recorded as goodwill.

Over a period of many years, this set of devices had in Olympus's accounts converted overvalued speculative assets into overvalued acquisitions; and the original speculative losses were invisible in the trail of transactions. The overvaluations were eventually corrected by impairment charges against purchased goodwill—¥55 billion in 2009 alone.

The sequence of acquisitions was prompted by a failure—losses on investments. Then the acquisitions themselves met our definition of failure—zero or negative operating gains combined with transaction costs. And ultimately (albeit after two decades) the strategy failed in its objective of misleading shareholders and other outsiders without suffering criminal charges.[4]

So two related rounds of M&A were deployed by Olympus (neither of which was concerned with achieving operating gains, and both of which will have imposed transaction costs at investors' expense). And sequences of acquisitions are the subject of Chapter 10. Integrating pre-merger devices with the manipulations available when recording an acquisition requires great skill and draws the admiration of fellow creative accountants. It can transform a series of failed mergers (on our definition) into a self-sustaining record of apparently profitable growth.

---

4   Directors were fined.

References

AAA (1991) American Accounting Association Committee on Accounting and Auditing Measurement, 1989–90, *Accounting Horizons*, 5(3), 81–105.

Abboud, L. (2021) Couche-Tard offer values Carrefour at just over $16bn. *Financial Times*, 14 January 2021, https://www.ft.com/content/c47ca582-6998-4de2-9050-d331aff59f9c.

Abboud, L. and Kirby, J. (2021) Couche-Tard's failed Carrefour bid sows investor doubts about France. *Financial Times*, 19 January 2021, https://www.ft.com/content/284c9d2b-9a27-4341-b332-c860cec07217.

Acharya, V., Bannerjee, R., Crosignani, M., Eisert, T. and Spigt, R. (2022) The making of fallen angels—and what QE and credit rating agencies have to do with it, *Federal Reserve Bank of New York, Liberty Street Economics*, 16 February 2022, https://libertystreeteconomics.newyorkfed.org/2022/02/the-making-of-fallen-angels-and-what-qe-and-credit-rating-agencies-have-to-do-with-it/.

Agrawal, A., Jaffe, J. and Mandelker, G. (1992) The post-merger performance of acquiring firms: A re-examination of an anomaly, *Journal of Finance*, 47, 1605–21.

Akerlof, G. (1970) The market for "lemons": Quality uncertainty and the market mechanism, *Quarterly Journal of Economics*, 84, 488–500.

Aliaj, O., Indap, S. and Kruppa, M. (2020) Spac sponsors prosper in '2020 money grab', *Financial Times*, 14 November 2020, https://www.ft.com/content/a5ff00fc-a2dd-49c7-a2bf-02bd6303a840.

Amel-Zadeh, A. (2020) Operating performance improvements after corporate takeovers: Fact or fallacy? in Amel-Zadeh and Meeks, eds (2020), *Accounting for M&A: Uses and Abuses of Accounting in Monitoring and Promoting Merger*, Abingdon and New York: Routledge, pp. 217–51.

Amel-Zadeh, A. and Meeks, G. (2019) Bidder earnings forecasts in mergers and acquisitions, *Journal of Corporate Finance*, 58, 373–92, https://doi.org/10.1016/j.jcorpfin.2019.06.002.

Amel-Zadeh, A. and Meeks, G., eds (2020) *Accounting for M&A: Uses and Abuses of Accounting in Monitoring and Promoting M&A*. Abingdon and New York: Routledge.

Amel-Zadeh, A. and Meeks, G. (2020a) Introduction, in Amel-Zadeh and Meeks, eds (2020), *Accounting for M&A: Uses and Abuses of Accounting in Monitoring and Promoting Merger*, Abingdon and New York: Routledge, pp. 1–9.

Amel-Zadeh, A., Faasse, J., Li, K. and Meeks, G. (2020) Stewardship and value-relevance in accounting for the depletion of purchased goodwill, in Amel-Zadeh and Meeks, eds (2020), *Accounting for M&A: Uses and Abuses of Accounting in Monitoring and Promoting Merger*, Abingdon and New York: Routledge, pp. 79–112.

Amel-Zadeh, A. and Meeks, G. (2020b) Earnings forecasts accompanying a bid, in Amel-Zadeh and Meeks, eds (2020), *Accounting for M&A: Uses and Abuses of Accounting in Monitoring and Promoting Merger*, Abingdon and New York: Routledge, pp. 142–71.

Amel-Zadeh, A., Meeks, G. and Meeks, J.G. (2016) Historical perspectives on accounting for M&A, *Accounting and Business Research*, 46(5), 501–24, https://doi.org/10.1080/0014788.2016.1182703.

Andrade, G., Mitchell. M. and Stafford, E. (2001) New evidence and perspectives on mergers. *Journal of Economic Perspectives*, 15, 103–20, https://doi.org/10.1257/jep.15.2.103.

Andre, P., Kooli, M. and L'Her, J.-F. (2004) The long-run performance of mergers and acquisitions: evidence from the Canadian stock market, *Financial Management*, 33(4), 27–43, https://www.jstor.org/stable/3666327.

Arnold, J., Egginton, D., Kirkham, L., Macve, R. and Peasnell, K. (1992) *Goodwill and Other Intangibles*, London: ICAEW.

Armstrong, R. (2020) Companies are dangerously drunk on debt, *Financial Times*, 7 May 2020, https://www.ft.com/content/e2d7f424-8eb6-11ea-9e12-0d4655dbd44f.

Asquith, P. (1983) Merger bids, uncertainty, and stockholder returns, *Journal of Financial Economics*, 11, 51–83.

Asquith, P. and Kim, E. (1982) The impact of merger bids on the participating firms' security-holders, *Journal of Finance*, 37(5), 1209–28.

Asquith, P., Bruner, R. and Mullins, D. (1983) The gains to bidding firms from merger, *Journal of Financial Economics*, 11, 121–39.

Ayres, C. (2002) $845m bonanza for Enron team, *The Times*, 18 June 2002.

Bach, L., Baghai, R., Bos, M. and Silva R. (2021) How do acquisitions affect the mental health of employees? Swedish House of Finance Research Paper No. 21–21, European Corporate Governance Institute — Finance Working Paper No. 793/2021, https://ssrn.com/abstract=3940462.

Bender, R. (2019) How Bayer-Monsanto became one of the worst corporate deals—in 12 charts, *Wall Street Journal*, 28 August 2019, https://www.wsj.com/articles/how-bayer-monsanto-became-one-of-the-worst-corporate-dealsin-12-charts-11567001577.

Beresford, D.R. (2001) Congress looks at accounting for business combinations, *Accounting Horizons*, 15(1), 73–86, https://doi.org/10.2308/acch.2001.15.1.73.

Binham, C. (2016) Watching the insiders, *Financial Times*, 21 May 2016, https://www.ft.com/content/4c07fe96-1d44-11e6-a7bc-ee846770ec15.

Black, F. (1986) Noise, *Journal of Finance*, 41(3), 529–43.

Blanes, F., de Fuentes, C. and Porcuna, R. (2019) Executive remuneration determinants: New evidence from meta-analysis, *Economic Research-Ekonomska Istraživanja*, 33(1), 2844–66, https://doi.org/10.1080/13316 77X.2019.1678503.

Boateng, A., Bi, X., and Brahma, S. (2017) The impact of firm ownership and board monitoring on operating performance of Chinese mergers and acquisitions, *Review of Quantitative Finance and Accounting*, 49(4), 925–48, https://doi.org/10.1007/S11156-016-0612-y.

Boswell, J. (1791/2008) *Life of Samuel Johnson*, London: Penguin Classics.

Botsari, A. (2020) Stock prices and earnings management around M&A transactions, in Amel-Zadeh, A. and Meeks, G., eds (2020), *Accounting for M&A: Uses and Abuses of Accounting in Monitoring and Promoting Merger*, Abingdon and New York: Routledge, pp. 115–41.

Botsari, A. and Meeks, G. (2008) Do acquirers manage earnings ahead of a takeover bid? *Journal of Business Finance and Accounting*, 35, 633–70, https://doi.org/10.1111/j.1468-5957.2008.02091.x.,

Botsari, A. and Meeks, G. (2018) Acquirers' earnings management ahead of stock for stock bids in 'hot' and 'cold' markets, *Journal of Accounting and Public Policy*, 37, 355–75, https://doi.org/10.1016/j.jaccpubpol.2018.09.007.

Bradley, M., Desai, A. and Kim, H. (1988) Synergistic gains from corporate acquisitions and their division between the stockholders of target and acquiring firms, *Journal of Financial Economics*, 21, 3–40.

Brooks, R. (2013) *The Great Tax Robbery: How Britain Became a Tax Haven for Fat Cats and Big Business*, London: Oneworld.

BT (2010) *Annual Report and Accounts*, http://www.btplc.com/Sharesand performance/Annualreportandreview/pdf/BTGroupAnnualReport2010.pdf.

Buffett, W. (1982) Letter to the Shareholders of Berkshire Hathaway, *Berkshire Hathaway*, www.berkshirehathaway.com/letters/1982.html.

Buffett, W. and Loomis, C.J. (1999) Mr. Buffett on the Stock Market (Fortune, 1999), *Fortune*, 22 November 1999, https://fortune.com/1999/11/22/warren-buffett-on-stock-market/.

Cable, J., Palfrey, J. and Runge, J. (1980) Federal Republic of Germany 1964–74, in Mueller, D., ed. (1980), *The Determinants and Effects of Merger: An International Comparison*, Cambridge, MA: Gunn and Hain, pp. 99–132.

Capron, L. (1999) The long-term performance of horizontal acquisitions, *Strategic Management Journal*, 20(11), 987–1018.

Capron, L. and Pistre, N. (2002) When do acquirers earn abnormal returns? *Strategic Management Journal*, 23, 781–94, https://doi.org/10.1002/smj.262.

Caves, R. (1989) Mergers, takeovers and economic efficiency: foresight vs. hindsight, *International Journal of Industrial Organisation*, 7(1), 151–74.

Chatterjee, R. and Meeks, G. (1996) The financial effects of takeover: accounting rates of return and accounting regulation, *Journal of Business Finance and Accounting*, 23, 851–68.

Chopra, N., Lakonishok, J. and Ritter, J. (1992) Measuring abnormal performance: Do stocks overreact? *Journal of Financial Economics*, 31(2), 235–68.

Collins, N. (2014) Common sense disappears when mining groups merge, *Financial Times*, 24 August 2014, https://www.ft.com/content/a6be7ca6-292c-11e4-8b81-00144feabdc0.

Collins, N. (2019) Big financial operators reap the rewards of Sainsbury's failure, *Financial Times*, 4 May 2019.

Comiskey, E. and Mulford, C. (2010) Goodwill, triggering events, and impairment accounting, *Managerial Finance*, 36(9), 746–67, https://doi.org/10.1108/0307435101106436.

Conn, R., Cosh, A., Guest P. and Hughes, A. (2005) The Impact on UK acquirers of domestic, cross-border, public and private acquisitions, *Journal of Business Finance and Accounting*, 32, 815–70, https://doi.org/10.1111/j.0306-686x.2005.00615.x.

Cornett, M. and Tehranian, H. (1992) Changes in corporate performance associated with bank acquisitions, *Journal of Financial Economics*, 31, 211–34.

Corrado, C. and Hulton, C. (2010) How do you measure a "technological revolution"? *American Economic Review, Papers and Proceedings*, 100, 99–104, https://doi.org/10.1257/aer.100.2.99.

Cosh, A., Hughes, A. and Singh, A. (1980) The causes and effects of takeovers in the United Kingdom: An empirical investigation for the late 1960s at the microeconomic level, in Mueller, D., ed. (1980), *The Determinants and Effects of Merger: An International Comparison*, Cambridge, MA: Gunn and Hain, pp. 227–70.

Crooks, E. (2018) GE bases strategy on "robust industrial logic", *Financial Times*, 27 June 2018, https://www.ft.com/content/8eab12bc-795c-11e8-bc55-50daf11b720d.

Crow, D. and Ward, A. (2016) Pfizer's long quest for tax inversion ends in failure, *Financial Times*, 2 April 2016, https://www.ft.com/content/bc90afe6-fc10-11e5-a31a-7930bacb3f5f.

Cumbo, J. and Wiggins, K. (2021) Axing of performance fees sought, *Financial Times*, 22 May 2021, https://www.ft.com/content/e9fae12d-17bc-47e3-80ad-b52d7e58fd2e.

Cunningham, C., Ederer, F. and Ma, S. (2018) Killer acquisitions, *Journal of Political Economy*, 129(3), 649–702, http://dx.doi.org/10.2139/ssrn.3241707.

Cuypers, I., Cuypers, Y. and Martin, X. (2017) When the target may know better: Effects of experience and information asymmetries on value from mergers and acquisitions, *Strategic Management Journal*, 38, 609–25, https://doi.org/10.1002/smj.2502.

Cyert, R. and March, J. (1963) *A Behavioural Theory of the Firm*, Englewood Cliffs, NJ: Prentice Hall.

Dargenidou, C., Gregory, A. and Hua, S. (2016) How far does financial reporting allow us to judge whether M&A activity is successful? *Accounting and Business Research*, 46(5), 467–99, https://doi.org/10.1080/00014788.2016.1182702.

Dasgupta, P. (2021) *The Economics of Biodiversity: The Dasgupta Review*, HM Treasury, https://www.gov.uk/government/publications/the-economics-of-biodiversity-the-dasgupta-review-government-response.

Dechow, P., Ge, W., Larson, C. and Sloan, R. (2011) Predicting material accounting misstatements, *Contemporary Accounting Research*, 28, 17–82, https://doi.org/10.1111/j.1911-3846.2010.01041.x.

Deloitte (2021) *Directors' remuneration in FTSE100 companies*, https://www2.deloitte.com/uk/en/pages/tax/articles/directors-remuneration-in-ftse-100-companies-oct-2021.html.

Dennis, D. and McConnell, J. (1986) Corporate mergers and security returns, *Journal of Financial Economics*, 16(2), 143–87.

Desbrieres, P. and Schatt, A. (2002) The impacts of LBOs on the performance of acquired firms: the French case, *Journal of Business Finance and Accounting*, 29(5), 695–729, https://doi.org/10.1111/1468-5957.00447.

Diaz, B., Olalla, J. and Azofra, S. (2004) Bank acquisitions and performance: Evidence from a panel of European credit entities, *Journal of Economics and Business*, 56(5), 377–404, https://doi.org/10.1016/jeconbus.2004.02.001.

Dickerson, A., Gibson, H. and Tsakalotos, E. (1997) The impact of acquisitions on company performance: evidence from a large panel of UK firms, *Oxford Economic Papers*, 49(3), 344–63.

Dickerson, A., Gibson, H. and Tsakalotos, E. (2000) Internal vs external financing of acquisitions: do managers squander retained profits? *Oxford Bulletin of Economics and Statistics*, 62(3), 417–31, https://doi.org/10.1111/1468-0084.00178.

Dissanaike, G. (1997) Do stock market investors overreact? *Journal of Business Finance and Accounting*, 24, 27–50.

Dissanaike, G. (2010) Are the world's major stock markets efficient? Implications for resource allocation and corporate governance in developing countries, in Kelegam, S. and Gunewardena, D., eds (2010), *Economic and Social Development under a Market Economy Regime in Sri Lanka*, pp. 17–32, https://www.ips.lk/wp-content/uploads/2017/01/Economic-Social-Development-Vol.II_.pdf.

Dissanaike, G., Jayasekera, R. and Meeks, G. (2022) Why do unsuccessful companies survive? US airlines, aircraft leasing, and GE, 2000–2008, *Business History Review*, forthcoming, https://ssrn.com/abstract=3966361.

Dodd, P. (1980) Merger proposals, management discretion and stockholder wealth, *Journal of Financial Economics*, 8(2), 105–37.

Dong M., Hirshleifer, D., Richardson, S. and Teoh, S.H. (2006) Does investor misvaluation drive the takeover market? *Journal of Finance*, 61, 725–62, https://doi.org/10.1111/j.1540-6261.2006.00853.x.

Drawbaugh, K. (2014) Burger King to save millions in US taxes in "inversion", *Reuters*, 11 December 2014, https://www.reuters.com/article/us-usa-tax-burgerking-idUSKBN0JP0CI20141211.

Duchin, R. and Schmidt, B. (2013) Riding the merger wave: Uncertainty, reduced monitoring and bad acquisitions, *Journal of Financial Economics*, 107(1), 69–88, https://doi.org/10.1016/jfineco.2012.07.003.

Eckbo, B. (1983) Horizontal mergers, collusion and stockholder wealth, *Journal of Financial Economics*, 11, 241–73.

Economist, The (2013) Goodwill Hunting, 14 May 2013, http://www.economist.com/blogs/schumpeter/2013/05/tata-steel.

Edgecliffe-Johnson, A. (2021) Equity should be offered to employees too, *Financial Times*, 6 September 2021, https://www.ft.com/content/636aef63-6b42-4d7b-9fd3-374289e4ec13.

Edgecliffe-Johnson, A., Silverman, G. and Fontanella-Khan, J. (2021) GE boss bids farewell to industrial complexity', *Financial Times*, 11 November 2021.

EFRAG/ASBJ/OIC (2014) *Should goodwill still not be amortised?* Discussion Paper, July 2014, https://www.efrag.org/Assets/Download?assetUrl=%2Fsites%2Fwebpublishing%2FSiteAssets%2FDP%2520Should%2520Goodwill%2520still%2520not%2520be%2520amortised%2520-%2520Research%25-20Group%2520paper.pdf&AspxAutoDetectCookieSupport=1.

Elder, B. (2021a) Online retailers are playing a risky game with the high street, *Financial Times*, 26 January 2021, https://www.ft.com/content/7194a1de-da9e-46b7-af06-a80d0a2cb9a1.

Elder, B. (2021b) Shareholder doubts escalate over LSE takeover of Refinitiv, *Financial Times*, 22 March 2021, https://www.ft.com/content/57b1b431-f897-47f8-a4c8-f4efdebefcfe.

Eley, J. (2021) Morrisons deal, *Financial Times*, 4 October 2021, https://www.ft.com/content/4d990b0f-2728-4126-adee-d4111aae7a45.

Elliott, J. A. and Shaw, W. H. (1988) Write-Offs as Accounting Procedures to Manage Perceptions, *Journal of Accounting Research*, 26, 91–119.

Engelberg, J., McLean, R. and Pontiff, J. (2018) Anomalies and news, *Journal of Finance*, 73(5), 1971–2001, https://doi.org/jofi.12718.

England, A. and Kerr, S. (2020) Gulf wealth funds embark on fishing expedition in a sea of cheap assets, *Financial Times*, 17 April 2020, https://www.ft.com/content/6079caf2-a9c2-4f9e-bf38-821549584cb4.

Ericson, M. and Wang, S. (1999) Earnings management by acquiring firms in stock for stock mergers, *Journal of Accounting and Economics*, 27, 149–76.

European Commission (2022) *Beyond GDP*, https://www.unescap.org/sites/default/d8files/knowledge-products/SD_Working_Paper_no14_May2022_Beyond_GDP_Global_Sustainability_Accounting.pdf.

Fama, E. (1970) Efficient capital markets: a review of theory and empirical work, *Journal of Finance*, 25, 383–417.

Felsted, A. and Agnew, H. (2014) Tesco Reels as Basket of Numbers Fails to Add Up, *Financial Times*, 23 September 2014, https://www.ft.com/content/5823a7cc-4279-11e4-9818-00144feabdc0.

Fernandes, N. (2019) *The Value Killers: How Mergers and Acquisitions Cost Companies Billions—and How to Prevent It*, Cham: Palgrave Macmillan.

Firth, M. (1979) The profitability of takeovers, *Economic Journal*, 89, 316–28.

Firth, M. (1980) Takeovers, shareholder returns, and the theory of the firm, *Quarterly Journal of Economics*, 94(2), 235–60.

Fleischer, V. (2020) Should we end the tax deductibility of business interest payments? *Financial Times*, 23 July 2020, https://www.ft.com/content/426c1465-9561-4300-8d3e-2430e4124c93.

Ford, J. (2018) Carillion's troubles were shrouded in a fog of goodwill, *Financial Times*, 18 June 2018, https://www.ft.com/content/765fc482-68db-11e8-b6eb-4acfcfb08c11.

Ford, J. (2019) Self-interest demands better policing of limited liability, *Financial Times*, 2 December 2019, https://www.ft.com/content/548705d2-1433-11ea-8d73-6303645ac406.

Ford, J. (2020a) Lockdown is exposing the folly of reckless financial strategies, *Financial Times*, 4 May 2020, https://www.ft.com/content/c8b72fa5-f15c-42b5-9613-fd9f14f012f3.

Ford, J. (2020b) Companies do not need any extra incentives to borrow, *Financial Times*, 13 July 2020, https://www.ft.com/content/377e5b23-c805-4bd1-ad8f-330ebc461572.

Foroohar, R. (2022) Where the Fed went wrong, *Financial Times*, 22 January 2022, https://www.ft.com/content/4133d4fd-3bf1-48c9-8e2f-249c9411f35c.

Franks, J. and Harris, R. (1989) Shareholder wealth effects of corporate takeovers: the UK evidence, *Journal of Financial Economics*, 23(2), 225–49.

FT Leader (2020a) Private equity groups do not need state help, *Financial Times*, 18 August 2020.

FT Leader (2020b) Taxing of private equity requires a rethink, *Financial Times*, 16 November 2020, https://www.ft.com/content/9968f554-f48b-44b6-b814-634901d6cb0e.

FT Leader (2021) Kravis, Roberts and private equity's record, *Financial Times*, 14 October 2021, https://www.ft.com/content/d78b8110-1ee7-4f21-bef7-d87ae09f051a.

FT Reporters (2016) Former Barclays director charged with leaking tips, *Financial Times*, 4 April 2016, https://www.ft.com/content/70bdb158-298e-11e6-8ba3-cdd781d02d89.

FT (2021) FT1000: Europe's Fastest Growing Companies, *Financial Times*, 22 March 2021, https://www.ft.com/reports/europes-fastest-growing-companies.

Galbraith, J. (1967) *The New Industrial State*, Princeton: Princeton University Press.

Galbraith, J. (1997) *The Great Crash of 1929*, Boston and New York: Mariner.

Galpin, T. and Herndon, M. (2014) *The Complete Guide to Mergers and Acquisitions: Process Tools to Support M&A Integration at Every Level*, San Francisco: Wiley.

GE (2001) *Annual Report 2000*, https://www.annualreports.com/HostedData/AnnualReportArchive/g/NYSE_GE_2000.pdf.

GE (2012) *Annual Report 2011*, https://www.annualreports.com/HostedData/AnnualReportArchive/g/NYSE_GE_2012.pdf.

Ghosh, A. (2001) Does corporate performance really improve following corporate acquisitions? *Journal of Corporate Finance*, 7, 151–87, https://dx.doi.org/10.1016/S0929-1199(01)00018-9.

Gong, G., Louis, H. and Sun, A.X. (2008) Earnings management. Lawsuits, and stock-for-stock acquirers' market performance, *Journal of Accounting and Economics*, 46, 62–77, https://doi.org/10.1016/j.jacceco.2008.03.001.

Goodhart, C. and Lastra, R. (2020) Equity finance: matching liability to power, *Journal of Financial Regulation*, 6(1), 1–40, https://doi.org/10.1093/jfr/fjz010.

Gregory, A. (1997) An examination of the long-run performance of UK acquiring firms, *Journal of Business Finance and Accounting*, 24, 971–1002.

Gregory, A. (2005) The long-run abnormal performance of UK acquirers and the free cash flow hypothesis, *Journal of Business Finance and Accounting*, 32, 777–814, https://doi.org/10.1111/j.0306-686x2005.00614.x.

Gregory, A. and Bi, X. (2011) Stock market driven acquisitions versus the Q theory of takeovers, *Journal of Business Finance and Accounting*, 38, 628–56, https://doi.org/10.1111/j.1468-5957.2011.02234.x.

Griffiths, I. (1986) *Creative Accounting*, London: Unwin.

Gryta, T. and Mann, T. (2020) *Lights Out: Pride, Delusion and the Fall of General Electric*, Boston: Houghton Mifflin Harcourt.

Gu, F. and Lev, B. (2011) Overpriced Shares, Ill-Advised Acquisitions, and Goodwill Impairment, *The Accounting Review*, 86(6), 1995–2022, https://doi.org/10.2308/accr-10131.

Guest, P., Bild, M. and Runsten, M. (2010) The impact of takeovers on the fundamental value of acquirers, *Accounting and Business Research*, 40(4), 1–20, https://doi.org/10.1080/00014788.2010.9663409.

Guthrie, J. (2020) Germany's corporations are in the dock, *Financial Times*, 2 July 2020, https://www.ft.com/content/e68d4353-60c5-44e9-b7a6-de01b38179ab.

Guardian, The (2004) Gent defends multi-million-euro bonuses, 26 March 2004, https://www.theguardian.com/business/2004/mar/26/executivesalaries.executivepay1.

Hannah, L. and Kay, J. (1977) *Concentration in Modern Industry*, London: Macmillan.

Harford, J. (1999) Corporate cash reserves and acquisitions, *Journal of Finance*, 54, 1969–997.

Harford, J. and Li, K. (2007) Decoupling CEO wealth and firm performance: The case of acquiring CEOs, *Journal of Finance*, 62(2), 917–49, https://doi.org/10.1111/j.1540-6261.2007.01227.x.

Hargreaves, D. (2019) *Are Chief Executives Overpaid?* Cambridge: Polity Press.

Hartzell, J., Ofek, E. and Yermack, D. (2004) What's in it for me? CEOs whose firms are acquired, *Review of Financial Studies*, 17(1), 37–61, https://doi.org/10.1093/rfs/hhg034.

Hauser, H. (2020) Arm sale will hit Europe's technological sovereignty, *Financial Times* (Letters), 24 August 2020, https://www.ft.com/content/4970848d-7821-45dc-b8cb-211036be5d30.

Healy, P., Palepu, K. and Ruback, R. (1992) Does corporate performance improve after merger? *Journal of Financial Economics*, 31, 135–76.

Healy, P., Palepu, K. and Ruback, R. (1997) Which takeovers are profitable? Strategic or financial? *Sloan Management Review*, Summer 1997, 45–57.

Helliwell, J., Layard, R. and Sachs, J. (2020) *World Happiness Report*, https://worldhappiness.report.

Hicks, J. (1935) Annual Survey of Economic Theory: The theory of monopoly, *Econometrica*, 3, 1–20.

Higgins, H.N. (2013) Do stock-for-stock merger acquirers manage earnings? Evidence from Japan, *Journal of Accounting and Public Policy*, 32, 44–70, https://doi.org/10.1016/j.jaccpubpol.2012.10.001.

Hill, A. (2019) Big corporate mergers take a hidden toll on staff, *Financial Times*, 15 September 2019, https://www.ft.com/content/d5bc4972-d546-11e9-a0bd-ab8ec6435630.

Hill, A. (2022) How to help your staff love a takeover threat, *Financial Times*, 14 February 2022, https://www.ft.com/content/4970848d-7821-45dc-b8cb-211036be5d30.

HMSO (1978) *A Review of Monopolies and Mergers Policy*, Cmnd. 7198, London: HMSO.

HoC (2012) *House of Commons Treasury Committee: The FSA's Report into the Failure of RBS*, HC640. London: The Stationery Office Ltd.

HoC (2016) *BHS, Report of the Work and Pensions and Business Innovation and Skills Committees*, HC 54, London: House of Commons, 25 July 2016.

HoC (2018) *Carillion, Report of the Business, Energy and Industrial Strategy and Work and Pensions Committees*, HC 769, London: House of Commons, 16 May 2018.

Hodgson, C. (2020) London looks at hopping on the Spacs bandwagon, *Financial Times*, 6 October 2020, https://www.ft.com/content/af75ce79-2bcd-46c4-92f4-8886513e539c.

IASB (2020) *Business Combinations—Disclosures, Goodwill and Impairment*, London: International Accounting Standards Board, 19 March 2020, https://www.ifrs.org/content/dam/ifrs/publications/discussion-papers/english/2020/-updated-dp-business-combinations-disclosures-goodwill-and-impairment.pdf.

Inagaki, K., Lewis, L. and Massoudi, A. (2020) Son's two weeks of turmoil at SoftBank, *Financial Times*, 6 April 2020, https://www.ft.com/content/d4ac5bad-c074-4335-a200-d821eda66632.

Indap, S. (2017) JPMorgan settles 2015 BlackBerry sale dispute, *Financial Times*, 2 June 2017, https://www.ft.com/content/fad85f16-df3a-3c2f-8e16-53d1307f3133.

Jenny, F. and Weber, A. (1980) France, in Mueller, D., ed. (1980), *The Determinants and Effects of Merger: An International Comparison*, Cambridge, MA: Gunn and Hain, pp. 133–62.

Jensen, M. (1986) Agency costs of free cash flow, corporate finance and takeovers, *AEA Papers and Proceedings*, 76(3), 323–29.

Jensen, M. and Ruback, R. (1983) The market for corporate control: the scientific evidence, *Journal of Financial Economics*, 11, 5–50.

Jensen, M. and Murphy, K. (1990) Performance pay and top management incentives, *Journal of Political Economy*, 98, 226–64.

Jones, M., ed., (2011) *Creative Accounting, Fraud and International Accounting Scandals*, Chichester: Wiley.

Keynes, J. M. (1936) *The General Theory of Employment Interest and Money*, London: Macmillan.

Knapp, M., Gart, A. and Becher, D. (2005) Post-merger performance of bank holding companies, 1987–1998, *Financial Review*, 40(4), 540–74, https://doi.org/10.1111/j.1540-6288.2005.00124.x.

KPMG (2014) *Who Cares About Goodwill Impairment?* http://www.kpmg.com/CN/en/IssuesAndInsights/ArticlesPublications/Documents/Who-cares-about-goodwill-impairment-O-201404.pdf.

Kumar, M. (1984) *Growth, Acquisition and Investment*, Cambridge: Cambridge University Press.

Kumps, A.-M. and Wtterwulghe, R. (1980) Belgium, in Mueller, D., ed. (1980), *The Determinants and Effects of Merger: An International Comparison*, Cambridge, MA: Gunn and Hain, pp. 67–97.

Kynaston, D. (2001) *The City of London, Volume 4: A Club No More, 1945–2000*, London: Chatto and Windus.

Lahey, K. and Conn, R. (1990) Sensitivity of acquiring firms' returns to alternative model specifications and disaggregation, *Journal of Business Finance and Accounting*, 17(3), 421–39.

Langetieg, T. (1978) An application of three-factor performance index to measure stockholder gains from merger, *Journal of Financial Economics*, 6(4), 365–83.

Leibenstein, H. (1966) Allocative efficiency vs "X-efficiency", *American Economic Review*, 56(3), 392–415.

Leonard, C. (2022) *The Lords of Easy Money: How the Federal Reserve Broke the American Economy*, New York: Simon and Schuster.

Lev, B. and Mandelker, G. (1972) The microeconomic consequences of corporate mergers, *Journal of Business*, 45(1), 85–104.

Lex (2017) Reckitt Benckiser: the daddy of payouts, *Financial Times*, 10 February 2017, https://www.ft.com/content/58661b28-ef94-11e6-ba01-119a44939bb6.

Lex (2021) Asda/Issa bros: dashboard fright, *Financial Times*, 22 October 2021, https://www.ft.com/content/b574e4ff-16d5-4280-8f45-a7c5fb5ae4f4.

Lex (2022) M&A/monetary Policy: quantitative pleasing, *Financial Times*, 18 February 2022, https://www.ft.com/content/0a177ae2-0fb5-41f1-bdfd-6ef22287f5e2.

Li, K. (2007) *Goodwill*, unpublished doctoral dissertation, University of Cambridge.

Limmack, R. (1991) Corporate mergers and shareholder wealth effects: 1977–1986, *Accounting and Business Research*, 21, 239–51.

Linn, S. and Switzer, J. (2001) Are cash acquisitions associated with better post-combination operating performance than stock acquisitions? *Journal of Banking and Finance*, 25(6), 1113–38, https://www.sciencedirect.com/science/article/abs/pii/S0378426600001084?via%3Dihub.

Loughran, T. and Vijh, A. (1997) Do long-term shareholders benefit from corporate acquisitions? *Journal of Finance*, 53, 1765–90.

Louis, H. (2004) Earnings management and the market performance of acquiring firms, *Journal of Financial Economics*, 74, 121–48, https://doi.org/10.1016/j.jfineco.2003.08.004.

Lugo, D. (2020) FASB to reintroduce amortization of goodwill for public companies, 18 December 2020, https://tax.thomsonreuters.com/news/fasb-to-reintroduce-amortization-of-goodwill-for-public-companies/.

Lynch, H. (1971) *Financial Performance of Conglomerates*, Cambridge, MA: Harvard University Press.

Lys, T. and Vincent, L. (1995) An analysis of value destruction in AT&T's acquisition of NCR, *Journal of Financial Economics*, 39, 353–78.

Ma, M., Sun, X., Waisman, M. and Yang, L. (2016) State ownership and market liberalization: evidence from China's domestic M&A market, *Journal of International Money and Finance*, 69, 205–23.

Malatesta, P. (1983) The wealth effect of merger activity and the objective functions of merging firms, *Journal of Financial Economics*, 11, 155–81.

Malmendier, U., Moretti, E. and Peters, F. (2018) Winning by losing: Evidence on the long-run effects of mergers, *Review of Financial Studies*, 31(8), 3212–64, https://doi.org/10.1093/rfs/hhy009.

Mandelker, G. (1974) Risk and return: The case of merging firms, *Journal of Financial Economics*, 1(4), 303–35.

Manne, H. (1965) Mergers and the market for control, *Journal of Political Economy*, 73(2), 110–20.

Marris, R. (1963) *The Economic Theory of Managerial Capitalism*, London: Macmillan.

Massoudi, A. (2016) AB InBev-SABMiller deal to yield $2bn in fees and taxes, *Financial Times*, 27 August 2016, https://www.ft.com/content/400e2334-6b6b-11e6-a0b1-d87a9fea034f.

Massoudi, A. and Abboud, L. (2019) How deal for SABMiller left AB InBev with lasting hangover, *Financial Times*, 24 July 2016, https://www.ft.com/content/bb048b10-ad66-11e9-8030-530adfa879c2.

Mauboussin, M. and Callahan, D. (2014) Capital allocation: evidence, analytical methods and assessment guidance, *Journal of Applied Corporate Finance*, 26(4), 48–74, https://doi.org/10.1111/jacf.12090.

Mauboussin, M. and Callahan, D. (2015) *Capital allocation updated: Evidence, analytical methods and assessment guidance*, Credit Suisse Global Financial Strategies, https://hurricanecapital.wordpress.com/2015/06/20/new-mauboussin-paper-capital-allocation-updated-evidence-analytical-methods-and-assessment-guidance/.

McKInsey & Company (2010) *Perspectives on Merger Integration*, June 2010, https://www.mckinsey.com/client_service/organization/latest_thinking/~/media/1002A11EEA4045899124B917EAC7404C.ashx.

Meeks, G. (1977) *Disappointing Marriage: A Study of the Gains from Merger*, Cambridge: Cambridge University Press.

Meeks, G. (2017) Understanding pension obligation figures, *British Politics and Policy at LSE*, 15 September 2017, http://eprints.lse.ac.uk/84689/.

Meeks, G. and Meeks, J.G. (1981a) Profitability measures as indicators of post-merger efficiency, *Journal of Industrial Economics*, 29(4), 335–44.

Meeks, G. and Meeks, J.G. (1981b) The case for a tighter merger policy, *Fiscal Studies*, 2(2), 33–46.

Meeks, G. and Meeks, J.G. (2013) Mergers, accountants and economic efficiency, *SSRN*, 26 December 2013, https://ssrn.com/abstract=2372028.

Meeks, G. and Meeks, J.G. (2020a) Managing earnings through M&A, in Amel-Zadeh, A. and Meeks, G., eds (2020), *Accounting for M&A: Uses and Abuses of Accounting in Monitoring and Promoting Merger*, Abingdon and New York: Routledge, pp. 172–88.

Meeks, G. and Meeks, J.G. (2020b) The impact of M&A on performance: Alternative measures of rates of profit, in Amel-Zadeh, A. and Meeks, G., eds (2020), *Accounting for M&A: Uses and Abuses of Accounting in Monitoring and Promoting Merger*, Abingdon and New York: Routledge, pp. 208–16.

Meeks, G., Meeks, J.G. and Meeks, P. (forthcoming) *Rising Inequality: The Contribution of Corporate Merger*.

Meeks, G. and Whittington, G. (1975) Directors' pay, growth and profitability, *Journal of Industrial Economics*, 24, 1–14.

Meeks, G. and Whittington, G. (2021) Death on the Stock Exchange: The fate of the 1948 population of large UK quoted companies, 1948–2018, *Business History*, https://doi.org/10.1080/00076791.2021.1893696.

Megginson, W., Morgan, A. and Nail, L. (2004) The determinants of positive long-term performance in strategic mergers: corporate focus and cash, *Journal of Banking and Finance*, 28, 523–52, https://doi.org/10.1016/S0378-4266(02)00412-0.

Minsky, H. (1986) *Stabilising an Unstable Economy*, New Haven: Yale University Press.

Mishan, E. (1967) *The Costs of Economic Growth*, London: Staples Press.

Moeller, S., Schlingemann, F. and Stulz, R. (2005) Wealth Destruction on a Massive Scale? A Study of Acquiring Firm Returns in the Recent Merger Wave, *Journal of Finance*, 60, 757–82, https://doi.org/10.1111/j.1540-6261.2005.00745.x.

Mueller, D., ed. (1980) *The Determinants and Effects of Merger: An International Comparison*, Cambridge, MA: Gunn and Hain.

Murphy, K. (1999) Executive compensation, in Ashenfelter, O. and Carl, D., eds (1999), *Handbook of Labor Economics*, Amsterdam: North Holland, pp. 2485–563.

Mulford, C. and Comiskey, E. (2005) *The Financial Numbers Game*, Chichester: Wiley.

Muolo, D. (2017) Former GE CEO Jeff Immelt used to have an empty private jet fly next to his just in case there were delays, *Business Insider*, 18 October 2017, https://www.businessinsider.com/ge-jeff-immelt-two-private-jets-2017-10?r=US&IR=T.

O'Dwyer, M. (2021) Deloitte partner pay touches 1million pounds as Big Four profits rebound, *Financial Times*, 22 September 2021, https://www.ft.com/content/2bb6e574-cd21-48fb-8660-7b93e4bf489b.

Olympus Corporation (2011) *The Third Party Committee, Investigation Report*, Olympus-global.com, 6 December 2011, https://www.olympus-global.com/en/common/pdf/if111206corpe_2.pdf.

Paterson, R. (1988) Fair value accounting following an acquisition, in Tonkin, D. and Skerratt, L., eds (1988), *Financial Reporting 1990–91: A survey of UK Reporting Practice*, London: ICAEW.

Peer, H. (1980) The Netherlands, in Mueller, D., ed. (1980), *The Determinants and Effects of Merger: An International Comparison*, Cambridge, MA: Gunn and Hain, pp. 163–91.

Penman, S. and Reggiani, F. (2014) The value trap: value buys risky growth, working paper, *Columbia Business School*, https://www.mygsb/faculty/resesarch/pubfiles/18184/Penman_value_trap.pdf.

Penrose, E. (1959) *The Theory of the Growth of the Firm*, Oxford: Basil Blackwell.

Perry, S. and Williams, T. (1994) Earnings management preceding management buyout. *Journal of Accounting and Economics*, 18, 157–79.

Pfeifer, S. and Milne, R. (2021) Norway blocks Rolls-Royce unit sale to Russians, *Financial Times*, 24 March 2021, https://www.ft.com/content/ef9ebc67-f542-4a99-8303-1792a1718780.

Phalippou, L. (2020) An inconvenient fact: Private equity returns and the billionaire factory, University of Oxford, Said Business School, Working Paper,https://ssrn.com/abstract=3623820.

Philippon, T. (2019) *The Great Reversal: How America Gave Up on Free Markets*, Cambridge, MA: Harvard University Press.

Pickard, J. (2021) Greensill link puts Heywood's role in spotlight, *Financial Times*, 24 April 2021, https://www.ft.com/content/78a63195-87c9-484c-8419-f9e9551e3498.

Pickard, J., Bradshaw, T. and Thomas, D. (2021) Regulations for foreign takeovers streamlined, *Financial Times*, 3 March 2021, https://www.ft.com/content/de604c4a-8df8-49b9-b76c-51f2b5f1e4df.

Pigou, A. (1920) *The Economics of Welfare*, London: Macmillan.

Plender, J. (2020) The seeds of the next crisis, *Financial Times*, 5 March 2020, https://www.ft.com/content/27cf0690-5c9d-11ea-b0ab-339c2307bcd4.

Powell, R. and Stark, A. (2005) Does operating performance increase post-takeover for UK takeovers? A comparison of performance measures and benchmarks, *Journal of Corporate Finance*, 11, 293–317, https://doi.org/10.1016/j.jcorpfin.2003.06.001.

Pratten, C. (1980) The manufacture of pins, *Journal of Economic Literature*, 18(1), 93–96.

Rahman, R. and Limmack, R. (2004) Corporate acquisitions and the operating performance of Malaysian companies, *Journal of Business Finance and Accounting*, 31(3–4), 359–400, https://doi.org/10.1111/j.0306-686x.2004.00543.x.

Ram, A. (2016) Tesco Probe Raises Supply Chain Concerns, *Financial Times*, 1 February 2016, https://www.ft.com/content/03c8b820-c5b3-11e5-808f-8231cd71622e.

Ramanna, K. and Watts, R. (2012) Evidence on the use of unverifiable estimates in required goodwill impairment, *Review of Accounting Studies*, 17(4), 749–80, https://doi.org/10.1007/s11142-012-9188-5.

Rangan, S. (1998) Earnings management and the performance of seasoned equity offerings, *Journal of Financial Economics*, 50(1), 101–22.

Rau, R. and Vermaelen, T. (1998), Glamour, value and the post-acquisition performance of acquiring firms, *Journal of Financial Economics*, 49(2), 223–53.

Ravenscraft, D.J. and Scherer, F.M. (1987), *Mergers, Sell-offs and Economic Efficiency*, Washington: Brookings.

Reference for Business (2022) *Fred A. Goodwin, 1959-*, https://www.referenceforbusiness.com/biography/F-L/Goodwin-Fref-A-1959.html.

Rennison, J. (2020) Private equity owners pile on leverage to reap dividends, *Financial Times*, 18 September 2020, https://www.ft.com/content/a9ff463b-01d7-4892-82dc-2dbb74941a16.

Robinson, E.A. (1931) *The Structure of Competitive Industry,* Cambridge: Cambridge University Press.

Ruddick, G. and Butler, S. (2017) Philip Green agrees to pay 363 million pounds into BHS pension fund, *The Guardian,* 28 February 2017, https://www.theguardian.com/business/2017/feb/28/ philip-green-agrees-pay-363m-bhs-pension-fund.

Ryden, B. (1972) *Mergers in Swedish Industry,* Stockholm: Amquist and Wicksell.

Ryden, B. and Edberg, J.-O. (1980) Large mergers in Sweden, in Mueller, D., ed. (1980), *The Determinants and Effects of Merger: An International Comparison,* Cambridge, MA: Gunn and Hain, pp. 193–226.

SAB Miller (2016), *Annual Report,* https://www.ab-inbev.com/content/dam/ universaltemplate/ab-inbev/investors/sabmiller/reports/annual-reports/ annual-report-2016.pdf.

Sandbu, M. (2019) More than a third of foreign investment is multinationals dodging tax, *Financial Times,* 8 September 2019, https://www.ft.com/ content/37aa9d06-d0c8-11e9-99a4-b5ded7a7fe3f.

Scherer, F.M. (1988) Corporate takeovers: the efficiency arguments, *Journal of Economic Perspectives,* 2(1), 69–82.

Scherer, M. and Ross, D. (1990) *Industrial Market Structure and Economic Performance,* Boston: Houghton Mifflin.

Schillit, H. and Perler, J. (2010) *Financial Shenanigans: How to Detect Accounting Gimmicks and Fraud in Financial Reports,* New York: McGraw Hill.

Schipper, K. (2010) How can we measure the costs and benefits of changes in financial reporting standards? *Accounting and Business Research,* 40(3), 309–27, https://doi.org/10.1080/00014788.2010.9663406.

Schwed, F. (1940/2006) *Where Are the Customers' Yachts?: Or a Good Hard Look at Wall Street,* Hoboken, NJ: Wiley.

SEC (2002a) *Securities and Exchange Commission v. Xerox Corporation,* Civil Action No 02 CV 2789 (DLC) (S.D.N.Y), April 11 2002, SEC Litigation Release No 17465, www.sec.gov/litigation.

SEC (2002b) Xerox settles SEC enforcement action charging company with fraud, 11 April 2002, https://www.sec.gov/litigation/litreleases/lr17465. html.

Segal, B. (2003) *Goodwill Write-Downs, SFAS No. 121, and the Adoption of SFAS No. 142,* unpublished doctoral dissertation, New York University, Stern School of Business.

Segerstrom, S. (2020) *Institutional ownership in the UK,* https://insight.factset. com/institutional-ownership-in-the-UK.

Sen, A. (1999) *Development as Freedom,* New York: Alfred Knopf.

Sherman, H, Young, S.D. and Collingwood, H. (2003) *Profits You Can Trust*, Hoboken, NJ: Prentice Hall.

Shiller, R. (2001) *Irrational Exuberance*, Princeton: Princeton University Press.

Shiller, R. (2015) *Irrational Exuberance*, Princeton: Princeton University Press.

Shleifer, A. and Vishny, R. (2003) Stock market driven acquisitions, *Journal of Financial Economics*, 70, 295–311, https://doi.org/10.1016/S0304-405X (o3)00211-3.

Singh, A. (1971) *Takeovers: Their Relevance to the Stock Market and the Theory of the Firm*, Cambridge: Cambridge University Press.

Singh, A. (1975) Takeovers, natural selection, and the theory of the firm: Evidence from the postwar United Kingdom experience, *Economic Journal*, 85, 497–515.

Smith, Adam (1776/1937) *An Inquiry into the Nature and Causes of The Wealth of Nations*, New York: Modern Library Edition.

Smith, R. and Wiggins, K. (2021) Asda buyers to stump up less than 800m pounds, *Financial Times*, 5 February 2021, https://www.ft.com/content/79964b33-2406-41c8-8f24-4ff5552f1669.

Smith, T. (1992) *Accounting for Growth: Stripping the Camouflage from Company Accounts*, London: Century Business.

Smith, T. (1996) *Accounting for Growth: Stripping the Camouflage from Company Accounts*, London: Random House.

Smyth, J. and Giles, C. (2021) OECD incoming chief confident of tax deal, *Financial Times*, 24 March 2021, https://www.ft.com/content/6adde5c7-ae73-417c-ae.42-0972e07d4982.

Somerset Webb, M. (2017) Time to reboot shareholder capitalism, *Financial Times*, 30 December 2017, https://www.ft.com/content/a99799d0-e648-11e7-a685-5634466a6915.

Song, G. and Meeks, G. (2020) The financial performance of acquired companies in the Chinese stock market, in Amel-Zadeh, A. and Meeks, G., eds (2020), *Accounting for M&A: Uses and Abuses of Accounting in Monitoring and Promoting Merger*, Abingdon and New York: Routledge, pp. 252–83.

Srivastava, A. (2014) Why have measures of earnings quality changed over time? *Journal of Accounting and Economics*, 57, 197–217, https://doi.org/10.1016/j.jacceco.2014.04.001.

Stafford, P. (2021) LSE's Schwimmer given 176% pay rise', *Financial Times*, 23 March 2021, https://www.ft.com/content/bbbf8294-a49e-4bd9-a4f1-d736f7080be3.

Stiglitz, J., Sen, A. and Fitoussi, J.-P. (2009) *Commission on the Measurement of Economic Performance and Social Progress*, https://www.ec.europa.eu/eurostat/documents/8131721/8131772/Stiglitz-Sen-Fitoussi-Commission.report.pdf.

Sudarsanam, S. and Mahate, A. (2003) Glamour acquirers, method of payment and post-acquisition performance, *Journal of Business Finance and Accounting*, 30, 299–341, https://doi.org/10.1111/1468-5957.00494.

Switzer, J. (1996) Evidence on real gains in corporate acquisitions, *Journal of Economics and Business*, 48, 443–60.

Tepper, J. and Hearn, D. (2019) *The Myth of Capitalism: Monopolies and the Death of Competition*, Hoboken, NJ: Wiley.

Tett, G. (2020) Bubble warning: Even college kids are touting Spacs, *Financial Times*, 9 October 2020, https://www.ft.com/content/e64c3e5e-b990-4904-adfe-139e41a5845b.

Thayer, E. (2010) Lehman say Barclays got $13billion windfall in sale, *Reuters.com*, 18 March 2010, https://www.reuters.com/article/us-lehman-barclays-idINTRE62H5K920100318.

Thomas, D. and Hollinger, P. (2021) Overseas buyers swoop to take bites out of UK plc, *Financial Times*, 1 March 2021, https://www.ft.com/content/79e6ec3e-e869-4c77-beef-938c306ed7bc.

Tobin, J. (1984) On the efficiency of the financial system, *Lloyds Bank Review*, 153, 1–15.

Tweedie, D. and Whittington, G. (2020) Developing new accounting standards for M&A: A standard-setters' perspective, in Amel-Zadeh, A. and Meeks, G., eds (2020), *Accounting for M&A: Uses and Abuses of Accounting in Monitoring and Promoting Merger*, Abingdon and New York: Routledge, pp. 57–78.

Tweedie, D., Cook, A. and Whittington, G. (forthcoming) *The UK Accounting Standards Board, 1990–2000: Restoring Trust and Honesty in Accounting*, Abingdon: Routledge.

Utton, M. (1974) On measuring the effects of industrial mergers, *Scottish Journal of Political Economy*, 21(1), 13–28, https://doi.org/10.1111/j.1467-9485.1974.tb00173.x.

Vandevelde, M. and Thomas, N. (2016). Tesco Criticized Over Treatment of its Suppliers, *Financial Times*, 27 January 2016, https://www.ft.com/content/5ba754af-dc7a-3d2b-a96b-8b5f020ebfb1.

Vandevelde, M. (2020) The leveraging of America, *Financial Times*, 10 July 2020, https://www.ft.com/content/c732fded-5252-4333-a3f8-80b767508bbc.

Vandevelde, M. (2021) Sprawling empires, *Financial Times*, 16 October 2021, https://www.ft.com/content/2c56a7da-6435-469c-90d8-28e966f20379.

Vincent, M. (2016a) Brexit leaves UK firms on the bargain shelf, *Financial Times*, 23 July 2016.

Vincent, M. (2016b) M&A bankers succeed in dodging the austerity bullet, *Financial Times*, 6 August 2016, https://www.ft.com/content/f6b6f454-5b07-11e6-8d05-4eaa66292c32.

Wade, R. (2020) It's time to change the rules for private equity (letter), *Financial Times*, 16 December 2020, https://www.ft.com/content/d5c04b77-cb3f-48ee-a53e-eb60007f119a.

Wiggins, K. (2020b) Stimulus helps private equity dealmaking hit fresh highs, *Financial Times*, 24 December 2020, https://www.ft.com/content/3091dd08-0301-424e-a049-7227a4883ef2.

Wiggins, K. (2021) Private equity chiefs wonder how much longer the good times can roll, *Financial Times*, 17 November 2021.

Wild, K. (1987) Merger accounting and goodwill, in Tonkin, D. and Skerratt, L., eds, *Financial Reporting 1986–87: A Survey of UK Reporting Practice*, London: ICAEW.

Wolf, M. (2015) *The Shifts and the Shocks: What We've Learned—And Still Have To Learn—From The Financial Crisis*, London: Penguin.

Wolf, M. (2021a) Now is the time to reform the UK's dysfunctional tax system, *Financial Times*, 8 February 2021, https://www.ft.com/content/06830ba4-2a50-4db1-93d0-3f03ce3d5350.

Wolf, M. (2021b) Economies can survive a market crash, *Financial Times*, 17 March 2021, https://www.ft.com/content/a8e8475a-c808-4552-96fb-7ce5551e338e.

Wu, T. (2018) *The Curse of Bigness*, New York: Columbia Global Reports.

Zeff, S. A. (2002) "Political" Lobbying on Proposed Standards: A Challenge to the IASB, *Accounting Horizons*, 16(1), 43–54, https://doi.org/10.2308/acch.2002.16.1.43.

Zhou, B., Guo, J., Hua, J. and Doukas, A. (2015) Does state ownership drive M&A performance? Evidence from China, *European Financial Management*, 21, 79–105, https://doi.org/10.1111/j.1468-036x.2012.00660.x.

Index

Index of Businesses

AB Inbev 51
ABN AMRO 36, 37
Alfred McAlpine 96, 97
Allergan 60
American Airlines 7
Arm Holdings 33, 34, 39, 75, 108, 128
Asda 34, 53, 65
AstraZeneca 60
AT&T 129
Audi 4
Autonomy 128, 131

Barclays 35, 42, 75
Bayer 29
Bear Stearns 64
Bergen Engines 108
Berkshire Hathaway 6, 21, 83
BHS 54, 55, 56, 97, 99
Blackstone 67
BP 129
Brunswick 34
BUPA 58
Burger King 59

Carillion 54, 81, 95, 96, 97, 98, 99, 100, 106, 125
Carlsberg 42
Carrefour 46
Cisco 81, 126, 129, 130
Clayton Dubilier and Rice 66
Coca Cola 81, 125
Coloroll 81, 91, 99, 130
Continental 7

Couche-Tard 46, 47
Credit Suisse 11
CVC 53
CVS Health 42

Debenhams 53
Delta 7
Duke Energy 42

EAGA 96
Enron 25, 81

Facebook 28, 128
Finsbury 34
Freshfields 34

GE 5, 9, 27, 36, 45, 63, 67, 81, 90, 91, 100, 101, 124, 125
Goldman Sachs 36, 100
Guinness 126, 130

Hanson 47
Heineken 42
HP 86, 128, 131

Instagram 28

JP Morgan 36, 39, 101

KKR 63
KPMG xvii, 86, 125, 131, 132

Lazard 34
Lehman 75
Linklaters 34, 57
LSE (London Stock Exchange) xvii, 24

Mannesmann 26, 57, 60, 85, 128, 131
McKinsey xi, 3, 59, 65, 112
Merrill Lynch 38, 53
Monsanto 29
Morgan Grenfell 40
Morgan Stanley 36, 101
Morrisons 66
Mowlem 96, 97

National Provincial 11
Ncipher 42
Northern Securities 40
Northwest 7
Nvidia 34, 108

Olympus 81, 132, 133, 134

Petsmart 42
Pfizer 60
Porsche 4
PwC xvii, 57

RAL 54
RBS (Royal Bank of Scotland) 4, 5, 9,
    36, 37, 38, 39, 109, 111
Reckitt Benckiser 25, 27
Refinitiv 24
Robey 34

Saatchi and Saatchi 130
SABMiller 33, 34
Sainsburys 34
Scania 4
Scottish and Newcastle 42
Seat 4

Shearer's Foods 66
Skoda 4
SoftBank 33, 34, 75, 128
Southwest 7
Spire 58
Symbol Technologies 130

TDR Capital 65
Tesco 29, 81, 127
Texas Pacific 53
Thales 42
Tim Hortons 60
Tiphook 130
TMH 108
Toys R Us 65

United Airlines 7
United Biscuits 47
US Airways 7
US Steel 39

Valeant 15
Viyella 39
Vodafone 26, 27, 57, 60, 85, 86, 128, 131
Volkswagen 4, 5, 9

Walmart 53
Westminster 11
WhatsApp 28
Wind Point Partners 66
WorldCom 81, 130

Xerox 81, 124

Subject Index

accounting manipulation 81, 132
accounting standards xvii, 77, 80, 81,
    91, 104, 109, 110, 126, 128, 129
advisers xi, 8, 12, 15, 16, 17, 21, 31, 33,
    34, 35, 36, 37, 38, 39, 40, 42, 43, 45,
    46, 47, 49, 50, 66, 77, 79, 95, 97, 98,
    99, 100, 103, 105, 109, 110, 111, 115

agency theory 132
amortisation 84, 85, 86, 87, 110, 128,
    129, 130, 132
anomalies 78, 87, 106, 110
antitrust 11, 15, 104, 108, 109
asymmetric monetary policy 50, 61, 96

audit xvii, 7, 8, 9, 79, 81, 84, 125, 126, 130, 131

bankruptcy 25, 54, 55, 64, 97, 105, 127
Brexit 75
bubble 41, 61, 74

capital gains 17, 50, 57, 58, 59, 67, 69, 75, 104, 106, 115
carried interest/carry 59, 67
central banks xii, 49, 50, 57, 61, 65, 66, 104, 107
channel stuffing 80, 90, 125
chief executives xvii, 24, 100, 113
concentration 96, 108
conglomerates 5, 63, 64, 67
consumer surplus 14, 15, 116
contracts xii, 26, 29, 53, 55, 80, 85, 90, 96, 98, 105, 106, 111, 123, 124, 125, 131
cookie jar 84, 91, 130
corporation tax 13, 50, 57, 58, 65, 104, 106
creative accounting 14, 17, 18, 53, 66, 69, 77, 78, 79, 80, 81, 82, 83, 84, 85, 86, 90, 91, 98, 100, 101, 104, 109, 110, 123, 124, 126, 127, 129, 132, 134
creditors 49, 50, 53, 98, 99, 103, 106
  unsecured 50, 106
cross-border takeovers 17, 50, 57, 107, 108

debt finance 10, 51, 65
deferred interest 126
deferred pay 55, 105, 112
disclosure 104, 109, 110, 131, 132, 133
dividends 10, 13, 48, 58, 63, 73, 77, 95, 98, 116
division of labour 3, 15
due diligence 38

earnings management 79, 82, 83, 110, 123, 124
earnings per share xvii, 4, 25, 26, 51, 52, 83, 85, 89, 90, 106, 124
efficiency xiii, 4, 5, 7, 15, 60, 71, 72, 73, 103, 106, 107, 108, 109, 110, 112, 113, 117

allocative 15, 107
informational 72
market 117
semi-strong. *See* semi-strong efficiency
employees 4, 6, 7, 8, 9, 33, 34, 35, 49, 50, 55, 56, 64, 79, 81, 97, 103, 105, 112
equity xvii, 10, 18, 36, 41, 46, 49, 51, 52, 53, 55, 59, 63, 64, 65, 66, 67, 68, 76, 77, 82, 96, 101, 103, 104, 105, 106, 109, 123. *See also* Private Equity; *See also* return on equity
event studies 116, 117, 118
executive jets 27, 100

failure (of merger) xi, xii, 3, 5, 11, 12, 13, 15, 17, 36, 37, 52, 53, 54, 68, 69, 72, 78, 81, 83, 90, 91, 95, 96, 97, 106, 111, 112, 113, 115, 129, 132, 133, 134
fair value 84, 90, 110, 127, 131, 132, 133
fallacy of composition 24
feedback loop 69, 78, 89, 101
financial engineering xi, 17, 18, 26, 49, 51, 64, 65, 66, 67, 105, 113
forecasts 69, 77, 79, 80, 83, 84, 86, 109, 117, 126
fraud 78, 79
front-loading 98, 124, 125
fund managers 46, 47, 48, 49, 75, 103, 105, 111

GDP xvii, 24, 30, 31
Goodhart's Law 26
goodwill 26, 80, 84, 85, 86, 87, 98, 110, 127, 128, 129, 130, 131, 132, 133, 136

impairment 78, 84, 85, 86, 98, 110, 129, 130, 131, 132, 133
incentives xi, 16, 17, 21, 23, 25, 27, 31, 33, 36, 45, 47, 48, 49, 52, 57, 58, 59, 64, 66, 67, 68, 77, 82, 86, 99, 100, 103, 105, 109, 111, 113, 132
information asymmetry xi, 18, 69, 74, 103, 104, 109, 113
insiders 41, 42, 43, 69, 76, 79, 81, 109
insider trading 42

intangibles 11, 78, 86, 87, 110, 128, 131
interest deductibility 57, 58, 65, 106. *See also* tax-deductible interest
interest-free funding 54, 97
investment banks xi, xii, 12, 31, 35, 39, 40, 41, 45, 46, 64, 111

leasing 53, 100, 124
limited liability 16, 17, 49, 52, 53, 54, 65, 68, 96, 105, 115, 116
lobbyists 29, 80, 87, 110, 129

monopoly 6, 7, 13, 14, 15, 16, 28, 95, 108, 115
monopsony 54, 95, 96, 108, 115
moral hazard 49, 51, 52, 53, 55, 56, 95, 96, 98, 104, 105, 106

NEDs (non-executive directors) xvii, 21, 39, 46, 49, 99, 104, 105, 109, 111, 112
negative equity 52

oligopoly 6, 7
operating gains xi, xii, 11, 17, 21, 43, 50, 60, 61, 68, 69, 72, 74, 75, 77, 89, 90, 103, 104, 108, 109, 111, 112, 113, 133, 134
overreaction 73
overvaluation 71, 74, 75, 77, 82, 109, 133

pensions 9, 47, 49, 53, 54, 55, 56, 63, 66, 95, 96, 97, 98, 99, 106, 111
performance-related pay xviii, 25, 34, 51, 90, 123
perks 23, 27, 41, 43, 100
premiums 9, 10, 41, 43, 47, 48, 53, 83, 111, 126, 127
price gouging 104, 107, 108
principal-agent problem 4, 64, 132
Private Equity xviii, 49, 50, 59, 63, 64, 65, 66, 67, 68, 90, 106. *See also* equity
public interest 108, 109

rent extraction 104, 105, 106, 107, 108, 112
rents 103, 104, 105, 106, 107, 108, 112, 131
reorganisation provision 99
return on equity 52
revised sequence 39, 40

scale economies 3, 6, 8, 11, 15
semi-strong efficiency 72, 79, 80, 81
serial acquirers 15, 27, 63, 78, 85, 89, 91, 99, 124, 125
share exchange 61, 75, 109
shareholders xviii, 4, 5, 9, 10, 12, 13, 14, 15, 16, 17, 18, 21, 23, 25, 26, 27, 28, 29, 31, 35, 39, 41, 43, 45, 46, 47, 49, 52, 57, 58, 64, 67, 72, 74, 79, 81, 82, 83, 96, 98, 101, 105, 109, 110, 111, 112, 113, 115, 116, 117, 118, 128, 129, 134
short-termism 48, 105, 111
SPACs xviii, 40, 41
speculative investment 78, 133
stewardship 4, 64, 128, 132
success fees 35, 110, 111
synergy 14, 15, 24, 83, 115

tax arbitrage 50, 59
tax avoidance 16, 60, 100, 101, 104
tax-deductible interest 57, 58, 65, 106. *See also* interest deductibility
tax inversion 60, 107
tax privilege 17, 29, 49, 50, 58, 59, 67, 68, 104, 106, 115, 116
total shareholder return xviii, 10
transaction costs 14, 24, 31, 33, 34, 77, 79, 115, 133, 134
turnaround takeover 4, 8, 11

voice/exit 46, 47

whistleblowers 78, 81, 127

About the Team

Alessandra Tosi was the managing editor for this book.

Melissa Purkiss performed the copy-editing, proofreading and indexing.

Katy Saunders and J. Gay Meeks designed the cover. The cover was produced in InDesign using the Fontin font.

Luca Baffa typeset the book in InDesign and produced the paperback and hardback editions. The text font is Tex Gyre Pagella; the heading font is Californian FB. Luca produced the EPUB, AZW3, PDF, HTML, and XML editions — the conversion is performed with open source software such as pandoc (https://pandoc.org/) created by John MacFarlane and other tools freely available on our GitHub page (https://github.com/OpenBookPublishers).

This book need not end here...

Share

All our books — including the one you have just read — are free to access online so that students, researchers and members of the public who can't afford a printed edition will have access to the same ideas. This title will be accessed online by hundreds of readers each month across the globe: why not share the link so that someone you know is one of them?

This book and additional content is available at:

https://doi.org/10.11647/OBP.0309

Donate

Open Book Publishers is an award-winning, scholar-led, not-for-profit press making knowledge freely available one book at a time. We don't charge authors to publish with us: instead, our work is supported by our library members and by donations from people who believe that research shouldn't be locked behind paywalls.

Why not join them in freeing knowledge by supporting us: https://www.openbookpublishers.com/support-us

Like Open Book Publishers

Follow @OpenBookPublish

Read more at the Open Book Publishers BLOG

You may also be interested in:

The Great Reset
2021 European Public Investment Outlook
Floriana Cerniglia, Francesco Saraceno, and Andrew Watt (eds)

https://doi.org/10.11647/OBP.0280

The Infrastructure Finance Challenge
Ingo Walter (ed.)

https://doi.org/10.11647/OBP.0106

Models in Microeconomic Theory ('She' Edition)
Martin J. Osborne and Ariel Rubinstein

https://doi.org/10.11647/OBP.0211

CPSIA information can be obtained
at www.ICGtesting.com
Printed in the USA
JSHW051559060722
27555JS00001BA/40

9 781800 647800